Creative Classroom Management
A Fresh Approach to Building a Learning Community

Grades K–2

by Dr. Sharon R. Lockett

Carson-Dellosa Publishing Company, Inc.
Greensboro, North Carolina

Dedication

To my friends, my family, and my PCA Dream Team
for sharing your ideas, support, encouragement, and
most of all, your love—"Doc"

Credits

Editor: Ashley Anderson
Layout Design: Van Harris
Inside Illustrations: Janet Armbrust and Lori Jackson
Cover Design: Peggy Jackson
Cover Photos: © Digital Vision® Ltd. All rights reserved.
© Photodisc

ISBN 1-59441-237-5

TABLE OF CONTENTS

Professional Resources

Canter, Lee, and Marlene Canter. *Assertive Discipline: Positive Behavior Management for Today's Classroom.* Santa Monica, CA: Canter and Associates, 1992.

Gibbs, Jeanne. *Tribes: A New Way of Learning and Being Together.* Windsor, CA: CenterSource Systems, LLC, 2001.

Marzano, Robert J., Jana S. Marzano, and Debra J. Pickering. *Classroom Management That Works: Research-Based Strategies for Every Teacher.* Association for Supervision and Curriculum Development, 2003.

INTRODUCTION

Whether in your second month or second decade of teaching, you have likely faced a time when it took all of the energy you could muster to simply walk into the classroom, face those challenging students, and begin to teach. The idea of standing before all of those energetic students who look to you to teach them can be very daunting. It can leave you wondering what to do to inspire future leaders to manage their behavior in a manner that will propel them into purposeful learning.

Accomplishing this goal is not achieved through a curriculum or program. There is no "one-size-fits-all" checklist for creating the perfect classroom. *Creative Classroom Management* does, however, offer a process that will help you develop a positive learning culture in the classroom community. A community classroom includes a well-implemented behavior management program and teaching/learning strategies that are geared toward increasing students' academic and social strengths. This method has the potential to impact not only their grades, but also their beliefs in their academic and social capabilities.

In this book, you will find a community-building approach, along with guidelines, strategies, applications, and activities to develop a community mind-set in the classroom. Effective and consistent utilization of these relationship-building strategies and discipline methods can help you create the "well-oiled machine" that you've always dreamed of. Enjoy the adventure!

> **Develop a positive learning culture in the classroom community and increase students' academic and social strengths.**

COMMUNITY IN THE CLASSROOM

Children today are amazing. They are brighter, more creative, more knowledgeable, and more sophisticated than ever before. Many of them have access to and regularly use technology. So, what can you offer them during the brief hours that you spend with them each day? What can you do to encourage them to participate, entice them to care about each other and their work, and involve them in the day-to-day events of the entire group? What can you offer that will make the classroom a haven of learning and a community of trust? Much more than you think! *It all begins with you!*

You can provide the positive learning community that they need. So, let's get started building the kind of classroom where every child has the opportunity to get to know his classmates and teacher, to help other members of the community, to care for them, and to celebrate them. Building a community within a classroom might be what you need to have an effective classroom management strategy!

What Is Community in the Classroom?

A classroom community asks students to build relationships with each other. Students who experience a sense of community in their classrooms and schools are much more likely to *want* to comply with behavioral expectations. They feel a sense of commitment and have positive relationships with their classmates and teachers. They don't want to let each other down.

Community in the classroom is a mind-set that focuses on students' emotional and social needs, as well as their intellectual needs. It is a commitment to providing a community atmosphere in the classroom, enabling each student to be more effective at accomplishing her academic goals. Even students who have difficult home situations can come to school knowing they will be supported and cared for in the safety of their classroom communities.

A community classroom supports students in making and sustaining connections with others. It connects children with each other and helps them learn about human interaction.

How Will Building a Sense of Community Benefit Me as a Teacher?

Think about your own personal relationships with your family, friends, and loved ones. They are part of your personal community. Why are they a part of your community? Probably because they positively influence you. You enjoy being in their presence. They have, in some manner, shown you that they care for you. This positive relationship with them makes you want to be cooperative, compliant, and caring. You take their advice, follow their directions, or seriously consider their suggestions primarily because you trust them. You believe that they give you advice, suggestions, and directions because they care.

The same concept applies to your ability to effectively manage students' behavior. The children who believe that you really care about them and their well-being will likely spend less time misbehaving because they prefer the feeling they have when you are pleased with their behavior.

Think about teachers who have students who are happy, as well as compliant. You will probably find that these teachers have learned strategies to effectively and appropriately befriend students and earn their trust while still maintaining a classroom structure and overall behavior plan. They understand the importance of capturing that special spirit of community. Good teachers recognize that children respond to realistic limits that are set in a clear, caring way. They understand that children learn best when they feel a sense of order.

> The children who believe that you really care about them and their well-being will likely spend less time misbehaving because they prefer the feeling they have when you are pleased with their behavior.

How Do I Build a Community Classroom?

You can accomplish this goal by regularly integrating strategies that help build a sense of community with specific strategies for managing student behavior in a positive yet effective manner. Implementing this process has the potential to make teaching and learning an even more pleasurable experience for both you and your students. A committed, community-building teacher recognizes the need to be deliberate in the effort to build such an atmosphere in the classroom.

What Are My Responsibilities in Creating the Community Classroom?

Within this book, you will find strategies, methods, and suggestions for tackling the challenge! All of these responsibilities will be discussed in depth later in the book. But, if you are looking for a quick checklist of reminders, you should remember the following five things.

1. Include families in the process.
2. Communicate calmly, clearly, and with authority.
3. Pay attention to positive behavior, as well as inappropriate behavior.
4. Say what you mean and mean what you say!
5. Be consistent with your expectations.

Communicate Your Expectations to Families.

In order for families to trust and support you, they need to get to know you, and you need to get to know them. Make every effort to establish relationships that show families how much you care about their children. It is important for families to know your expectations for student behavior. The sooner you communicate your expectations and begin forming relationships with families, the better.

Get in Touch with Families during the Summer: After you receive the class list for the year, begin planning. Don't wait for the first day of school to start establishing relationships. It's never too early to get off to a good start!

Personal Visits

If possible, a brief visit with each family can give you powerful information that you could never glean any other way. While it does require a sacrifice of your time and energy, it will be beneficial to you as the year progresses. When you tell a family that you would like to meet with them outside of the school and before summer vacation has even ended, you let them know that you really care about them and will take special interest in their child.

Use a city map to assist you in scheduling the visits. Contact each family to establish a good meeting location—a restaurant, a park, or even the family's home—anywhere that is a mutually acceptable location. Try to visit three families each day. If you coordinate your plans to visit families who live in the same area, you will significantly decrease travel time each day. Allot approximately one hour per visit.

Tips for Success:

- Consider taking someone with you (a spouse or a friend) to increase your comfort and success.

- Take a few mementos with you, such as a picture you drew when you were the student's age, one of your own school pictures, something that represents a hobby or your favorite thing to do, or pictures of your family members or pets.

- Give the student a new pencil to save until the first day of school or to use during the summer to remember you.

- Give the family a packet that might contain a class calendar listing school and classroom events, an invitation to visit the classroom, and a school or classroom handbook filled with important information for parents and students to review.

- Use game strategies to get to know a child. Take a small rubber ball and use it as a tool to get a shy child to interact with you. For example, hide the ball behind your back and let the child guess where it is. Or, take a set of manipulatives to find out if the child can demonstrate one-to-one correspondence and/or put together sets showing 2 + 4, 7 − 3, etc. This will not only give you information about the child's conceptual abilities, but you will also be able to assess verbal skills as you get to know each other. Additionally, this time gives you an opportunity to see how well the child interacts with you and with family members.

"I Care" Packages

If personal visits are not a realistic option for you, consider creating an "I Care" Package for each student. Write a letter on school stationery in which you introduce yourself to the class and welcome them to the classroom community. Specify some of the fun activities they will complete during the year, some of your favorite things to do, and any other information that you might like to share. Be sure to include a picture of yourself. Send a copy of the letter and picture to each child, along with a small gift, such as a pencil, a coloring book, a pack of crayons, a storybook, or a small toy. Students will be excited to receive their packages in the mail. This will make a great early connection for you and your students, and you will impress their families with your effort to pay personal attention to their children.

"Before School Starts" Letter

Early communication with families is critical to classroom community success. Begin with a letter written on school stationery to introduce yourself and express your positive attitude toward building community among students. Send the letter during the summer, just before school starts. This makes a positive impression on families and opens the door for them to support the community-building process. Following is a sample introductory letter (page 10). Use it as a template or alter it to fit your needs. This letter can be used as a part of the "I Care" Packages if you want to include a note directed to the families, as well as the students.

Sample Introductory Letter

Dear Family of _____,

I am thrilled that I will be working with you and _____ this school year. I think of our classroom as not just a classroom but a community that includes students, families, teachers, and administrators. In our community, we learn to care about each other and work together. Our community celebrates every member of the group. We are happy to have you and _____ joining us.

This is my _____ year of teaching, and I find each year to be more exciting. I love watching children learn and prosper in a caring, community-oriented environment. I am committed to keeping in contact with you throughout the year because you are the most important people in your child's life. You are welcome in our community whenever you would like to visit. You do not need to make an appointment.

If I can assist you in any way to make this the best year _____ has ever had, please feel free to call and leave a message for me. I will call you back at my earliest convenience.

Thank you for trusting me with your child. As the leader of our classroom community, I am dedicated to giving _____ the best learning experience possible. You are a very important part of our classroom community, and I look forward to your participation and input.

Sincerely,

_____

"Beginning of the Year" Phone Call

A "Beginning of the Year" Phone Call is another way to establish a relationship with each family. Often, a phone call from a teacher indicates bad news. So, imagine the surprise when a family member receives a positive phone call from you before school starts or during the first week of school! Taking time to make these calls will benefit you as the year progresses in the classroom community.

The purpose of these phone calls is to get acquainted with and introduce yourself to students' families. Following is a sample phone call script (page 12). Before you call, adapt the script to meet your specific needs. Also, consider sending the "Before School Starts" Letter before you make this call. Include in the letter that you will be calling so that family members will feel more comfortable and prepared to talk to you. If you are not sending a letter home, be sure to explain the concept of a classroom community during the phone conversation. Consider adding some of the information from the Sample Introductory Letter (page 10) when you adjust the phone call script.

During the phone call, document the conversation by taking notes to keep a record of any important information. This will help you remember important issues and impressions that you glean about each child and her family.

Tip for Success: This phone call is *not* the time to bring up concerns about a student. This should be a totally positive, relationship-building activity.

Later in the school year, you may find it necessary to make a phone call to help correct a student's behavior or work ethic, but you will have increased the possibility of gaining the family's support if they have already had a positive phone experience with you. This early interaction will be beneficial for you and the students.

Note: If you do not feel comfortable making phone calls, adapt the script to create a "Getting to Know You" Questionnaire to send home to families. Mail the form with the "Before School Starts" Letter or send it home with students on the first day of school.

Sample Phone Call Script

Hello, this is _____ ,

I am _____'s teacher for this year. I just called to let you know how delighted I am to have him/her in our community. We will have a wonderful year together.

To help us get off to a good start, can you tell me some things about _____ so that I can get to know him/her better?

- Favorite color: _____

- Favorite toy or game: _____

- Likes about school: _____

- Dislikes about school: _____

- Favorite thing to do after school: _____

- Favorite music: _____

- Is there anything you think I should know about him/her to help us have a fantastic school year?

    _____

    _____

That's great! Well, let me tell you a little bit about myself and why I am so excited to have _____ in our community this year.

- *Note some thoughts you want to share with the family member about yourself here:*

    _____

    _____

It's been a pleasure speaking with you. Please remember that you are always welcome in our classroom. We value the participation of all of our community members, and that includes our families.

- *Other ideas/notes:* _____

    _____

The First Day of School: Talk About the Word *Community*.

Begin creating your classroom community on the first day of school. Talk with students about the word *community*. Ask them what they think the word means. You will likely receive some bizarre answers and some that might actually touch on the real meaning of the word. It is important for you to define *community* for the class. Help students understand that a community is a group of people with some common interests and ideas who spend time together on a regular basis. Community members work to make life more enjoyable for each other.

Have students suggest other groups that might be communities based on the definition that you have discussed. Lead them through this discussion and help them see that each of their families is a community and so is the class.

Ask students a question, such as, "What do we need to do to make a fun, awesome community?" Then, tell them, "This year, we will create an awesome community right here in our own classroom!" Use this time as a chance to begin brainstorming ways to create a community. Ask students for suggestions about positive things that will make the classroom a better place. Help them by leading the discussion and, if necessary, suggesting ways to build positive relationships, such as following directions, being respectful of each other at all times, not calling people names, complimenting each other on a job well done, etc.

A community is a group of people with some of the same interests and ideas who spend time together on a regular basis. Community members work to make life more enjoyable for each other.

The members of a positive classroom community should get to know each other well. Place an emphasis on having children remember important facts about each other. It feels good to be in a place where you feel secure and included, where other people care about your interests, hobbies, likes, and dislikes. Children who feel this way are less likely to misbehave because their needs for attention and caring are being met, not only by you, but also by their peers.

This chapter includes a variety of icebreaker activities that can be used at the beginning of the year. They are also useful throughout the year to keep in touch with the changes in each student's life. Children never get tired of these activities because the results are often different, and they learn so much about themselves and their peers. This will help develop a sense of security among the children and reduce their desire to misbehave as a means of getting attention.

During the first month of school, use one icebreaker activity each day. After that, plan to use one each week. While this may seem to be a poor use of time in an already crowded schedule, it will actually prove to be a time-saver by minimizing the behavior problems that take up so much valuable time.

Choices

Supplies: several colorful carpet squares, place mats, or large sheets of laminated construction paper

Sorting Suggestions:

- Favorite color
- Favorite type of pet
- Favorite thing to do outside
- Favorite toy
- Favorite food
- Favorite quiet thing to do
- Favorite noisy thing to do
- Favorite place to go with your family

Directions: Choose one of the sorting suggestions on page 14 or one of your own. For example, tell students that the category is "favorite color." Explain that there are carpet squares on the floor that represent several colors. Instruct each student to choose a favorite color in his mind. Then, when you call his name, he should go to that square and stand beside it. Remind students that this is not a time to share their thoughts with each other. They are simply showing their personal choices by walking to the carpet squares and standing quietly. Having students move to specific places (carpet squares or place mats) allows them to visually demonstrate their preferences. Explain that when they move to their chosen places, they must stay there and may not change their minds.

When all of the children have settled on favorites, ask them to sit on the floor with their groups. Have them look at the community members who like the same color. Let them take a few minutes to talk about why they made their choices and find some commonalities among group members.

Always encourage students to listen carefully to what their classmates say about their choices. As a conclusion to this activity, ask some "remembering questions," such as, "Raise your hand if you remember William's favorite color?" "Who can name one student who stood by the red square?" "Which other students said that they liked the same color as William?" "Who remembers how many students stood beside the blue square?"

Conclude this debriefing with a statement of acceptance, such as, "Wow, a lot of our community members like the same colors, and a lot like different ones. I appreciate all of our similarities and differences. What a great community classroom we have!"

Keep referring to the classroom as a community. It will help build a more positive and well-managed teaching and learning environment.

Note: As you use different topics for this activity, draw or cut out magazine pictures to put on top of the squares to indicate choices. For example, a "Favorite Types of Pets" game might include carpet squares that feature pictures of dogs, cats, hamsters, fish, lizards, birds, etc.

Bingo

Following are directions for two versions of Bingo. If you choose to use the game cards for "Things I Like to Do" Bingo (page 18) or "I Might Like to Be" Bingo (page 19), use the first set of directions. If you choose to have students make their own Bingo cards, use the blank game card (page 20) and the second set of directions.

Supplies: one Bingo card and space markers (coins, small squares of construction paper, etc.) for each student, resealable plastic bag, scissors

Directions for "Things I Like to Do" and "I Might Like to Be" Bingo: Copy the selected game card onto sturdy paper and laminate for durability. Make one copy for each student. Make an additional copy of the game card and cut apart the squares. Place these game pieces in a resealable plastic bag.

Draw one game piece from the bag. Call out the name of the item pictured on the piece. A student should place a marker over that space on her Bingo card only if that square applies to her. For example, if you are playing "Things I Like to Do" Bingo and you call out, "ride a bike," a student who likes riding a bike would cover that space. A student who does not like to ride a bike would not cover the space. If you are playing "I Might Like to Be" Bingo, tell students to cover any occupation that might interest them when they grow up even if they already know what they want to be. Play continues until a student gets five in a row and calls out, "Bingo!"

Now, here's the important part—have the winning child read what he has covered with each space marker. As he does this, repeat the child's answers and interact very briefly with the class about the similarities and differences between their choices and the winner's choices. It might sound something like this:

"Marcus, you like to read? That's a great hobby. Students, stand up if you also like to read." (They stand up.)

"Marcus, help me name the people in our class who also like to read." (As he calls his classmates' names, they sit.)

This will provide a connection between classmates and their peers, as well as help students learn their new classmates' names. The emphasis is placed on finding similarities and differences and celebrating both.

Continue this type of interaction for each of Marcus's winning game pieces. Children have a strong need to know and be known by others. This game assists with the process.

Directions for Using the Blank Bingo Card: Before you begin the activity, select a topic for the game, such as "Favorite Foods," "Favorite Games," "Places I'd Like to Visit," etc. Copy the blank game card onto sturdy paper. Make one copy for each student. Distribute the game cards.

Conduct a brainstorming session with the class. Have students suggest possible items to fill the spaces on their cards. For example, if the game is "Favorite Foods," they might suggest pizza, apples, ice cream, peanut butter and jelly sandwiches, carrots, etc. List these items on the board. Then, help students fill in their game cards with the favorite foods that they would like to include. Explain that they can also include items that are not on the list. When all of the cards are complete and students are ready to play, distribute the space markers.

Instead of calling out items yourself, let students take turns calling out items from their own cards. This will provide an opportunity for students to interact during the game and will help them realize that other classmates selected some of the same items for their own cards. When a student calls out, "Bingo," proceed with the interaction described on page 16. Take time to discuss some of the unique items included on students' game cards.

Variation for Blank Bingo Cards: After students have filled in their game cards, make the game more interactive! Instruct students to walk around the room looking for classmates who have matching items written on their game cards. When a student finds a classmate with a match, each student should initial the other student's matching square. Explain that each student can only mark one square on another student's card, but more than one student can mark in a square. In other words, students can have multiple signatures in one square. But, they cannot have duplicate signatures on their cards.

For example, Suzie and Paulo might mark "pizza" on each other's "Favorite Foods" game cards. They wouldn't be able to mark any other common squares. (This is to prevent students from signing other cards multiple times.) They would then go to other classmates to look for more matches. If Suzie found that Meghan also had "pizza" on her card, Meghan could sign Suzie's card even though Paulo already signed the "pizza" square.

Encourage students to interact during this activity and ask questions to find out how they are alike and how they are different. After students have had time to talk with most or all of their classmates, have them return to their seats. Discuss and celebrate their similarities and differences. This version of the game focuses on building relationships. Unlike traditional Bingo, there will not be a single "winner" in this game.

Things I Like to Do

B I N G O

ride a bike	go for a walk	paint a picture	play with a pet	sing
make cookies	dance	put together a puzzle	play a game	play outside
play a sport	read or listen to a story	FREE	run a race	go fishing
eat pizza	go to a party	play computer games	play with friends	do math problems
go on a trip	go to school	do arts and crafts	swim	watch TV

CD-104117 Creative Classroom Management

I Might Like to Be

BINGO

B	I	N	G	O
librarian	doctor	farmer	police officer	lifeguard
mail carrier	grocer	veterinarian	bus driver	plumber
reporter	parent	FREE	teacher	principal
judge	dentist	construction worker	mayor	chef
author	firefighter	pilot	coach	nurse

B	I	N	G	O
		FREE		

CD-104117 Creative Classroom Management

Friend Venn Diagrams

Supplies: copy of the Friend Venn Diagram (page 22) and pencil or marker for each pair of students

Directions: Seat students in a group in front of the board. Choose a topic, such as favorite colors, favorite foods, favorite school subjects, favorite things to do when not in school, favorite television shows, etc. Then, select two students to demonstrate how to make a Venn diagram. Have them stand with you in front of the class. Draw a large Venn diagram on the board. Title the diagram and label the three sections. For example, the title might be "Favorite Colors," and the section labels might be "Jamie likes," "Kelsey likes," and "We like." Have Jamie and Kelsey help you fill in the Venn diagram. (See the sample illustration below.)

After you demonstrate the process of making a Friend Venn Diagram, divide students into pairs and have them create their own Friend Venn Diagrams. First, have them fill in the title and labels in the appropriate blanks. Then, have them talk with their classmates to discover their similarities and differences. They will enjoy learning more about each other. Conclude the exercise with a discussion focusing not only on what students learned about each other, but also on how important it is to get to know the members of the classroom community. This is a useful activity throughout the year and can even be used for problem-solving situations. (To facilitate problem solving, label the sections of a Venn diagram "_____ thinks," "_____ thinks," and "We think." Have students fill in the sections to find common ground and get the discussion started.)

Friend Venn Diagram

Title: _____

:: _____

:: _____

We

Memory Magic

Directions: Seat students with you on the floor in a circle. Choose a question for the game and share it with the class. For example, the question might be, "What is the name of one of your siblings?" Select one student to start the game. For example, if that student is John, he will say, "My brother's name is Ted." The student next to John, Brian, will say, "My sister's name is Claire. John's brother's name is Ted." The next student, Martina, will say, "I'm an only child. Brian's sister's name is Claire. John's brother's name is Ted." This continues until everyone in the circle has taken a turn. The goal is to see who has the best memory. When several students have taken turns, they might need to help each other remember the long list of names! However, the important part of this game is for students to learn to listen well and remember what is being said. It also encourages them to get to know each other.

Here are a few possible questions to use, or you can create your own.

- What is your favorite season?
- What do you like to do in the winter (spring, summer, fall)?
- What is your favorite game to play?
- What is your favorite animal?
- What is the name of one of your pets?
- What do you love about school?
- What is your favorite book?
- What does your family do for fun?
- What is your favorite TV show?
- If you had 10 dollars, what would you buy with it?

The VIP (Very Important Person) System

Supplies: sturdy bag that closes tightly, such as a cloth shoulder bag with a zipper, a child's backpack, or a child-sized rolling suitcase; special VIP chair to place in front of the class

Directions: Write each student's name on a craft stick and place the sticks in an empty jar or can. At the end of the first day of school, explain that one community member will get to take home the VIP bag each day. Draw a craft stick from the jar and give that child the VIP bag. Instruct her to take the bag home and place three to five small items inside it. The items should be important to the child. All of the items must fit in the bag when it is closed securely. Items might include a favorite book, a picture of the child's family, a favorite toy, a picture she has painted, etc.

The next day, the VIP will sit in the VIP chair and share her very important items with the community. This will help the other children know special things about the VIP. As soon as sharing time has ended, the child should return her VIP items to her desk or cubby for safekeeping until the end of the day.

For the remainder of the day, the VIP can enjoy special privileges, such as wearing a special VIP badge (below), serving as the line leader, passing out papers, acting as your helper, etc.

At the end of the day, select a new student to take home the VIP bag and be the next VIP.

Continue until every student has had a chance to be the VIP.

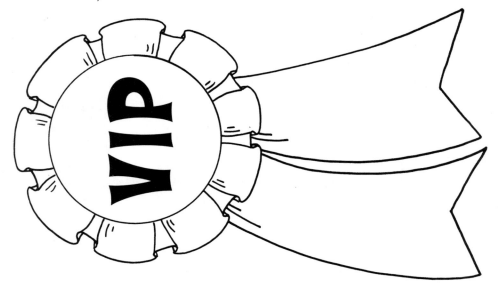

Lining Up

Children love to have special places in line. Establish different methods of lining up that allow the children to learn more about their classmates.

Directions: Instruct students, "You may get in line if you _____." Fill in the blank with various phrases until everyone is in line. Here are some suggestions:

Get in line if you . . .

- have an older (or younger) brother or sister.
- are an only child.
- have a pet.
- like to draw animals.
- like to eat carrots.
- can ride a bike without training wheels.
- have a birthday in March.

Student Interviews

Supplies: one copy of an interview sheet (pages 26–27) for each student, pencils, crayons

Directions: Choose one of the two interview sheets based on students' reading and writing abilities. Divide the class into pairs. Distribute one copy of the interview sheet to each student. Each student should interview his partner and fill out the sheet. After he is finished, his partner should interview him and fill out her sheet.

Remind students to focus their attention on their partners, taking special note of the responses to the interview questions.

When the interviews are complete, have students return to their seats so that you can discuss the interview results as a class. Ask each child to tell the most interesting thing he learned about his partner. Or, select two or three questions from the interview sheet and ask each child to share her partner's responses to those questions.

This activity can be repeated once or twice a month with different partners so that each child can get to know other classmates.

Student Interview

Name: _____

I am interviewing: _____

Directions: Ask your partner the questions. Circle your partner's answers.

1. What does your partner like to do at school?

2. What does your partner like to eat?

3. What does your partner like to do at home?

 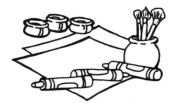 

4. Color in the oval with your partner's favorite color.

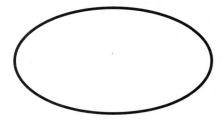

Student Interview

Name: _____

I am interviewing: _____

Directions: Ask your partner the questions. Write your partner's answers on the lines.

1. What are your partner's three favorite foods? _____

_____

_____

2. What are your partner's three favorite TV shows? _____

_____

_____

3. What are your partner's three favorite toys or games? _____

_____

_____

4. What are your partner's three least favorite foods? _____

_____

_____

5. What makes your partner proud of himself/herself? _____

_____

Scramble-Unscramble

Supplies: camera, one resealable plastic bag for each child in class, stapler or tape, sentence strips, permanent marker

Directions: Take a picture of each student. Staple or tape each picture to the front of a resealable plastic bag. Use a permanent marker to neatly write each child's name below her picture. Then, print each child's name on a sentence strip, leaving enough space between the letters to cut them apart. Cut apart the letters so that there is one letter on each piece of sentence strip. Put the letters inside the corresponding plastic bags and seal them.

Have students sit at their desks or on the floor in a circle. Give each student a plastic bag with a classmate's picture on it. Instruct each child to remove the letter pieces from the bag and use the picture as a clue to help her arrange the letters to form her classmate's name. Tell students to use the names on the fronts of the bags to check their work. When students have completed the names in front of them, instruct them to scramble the letters, stand up, and find new seats. They should then sit and begin to unscramble the new names in front of them.

Tip: After you have used this game as a whole-group activity a few times, place the bags in a center and allow children to play on their own when time allows.

We Fit Together Perfectly

This is a great activity for the first day of school because it demonstrates the importance of each student to the group. When one member is missing, the group is not complete.

Supplies: two pieces of poster board, black marker, scissors, stapler, markers/crayons

Directions: Draw the cut lines for a puzzle on one piece of poster board. Make sure to draw one puzzle piece for each student in the class, as well as one for yourself. Cut apart the puzzle pieces. Then, create a guide for assembling the puzzle by using the marker to trace each puzzle piece onto the second sheet of poster board. Staple the guide to a bulletin board and title it "We Fit Together Perfectly in Ms. Bonnett's Room."

On the first day of school, give each child a puzzle piece. Instruct students to write their names on their puzzle pieces. Then, they should use markers or crayons to decorate their pieces. When a child completes her design, help her find where her piece belongs on the bulletin board and staple it in place. When the puzzle is complete, have a class discussion about the importance of being unique but also working together as a whole group.

"I Am Very Special" Collage

Supplies: a variety of magazines; one envelope for each child, labeled with his name; one piece of large construction paper for each child; child's scissors; glue

Directions: Spend some time talking with students about being unique. Explain that no two people in the world are exactly alike. Each member of the classroom community is special and talented in his own way. Some of us like to spend time outdoors, while others prefer to be indoors. Some of us have big families, while others do not. We are unique in the foods we love to eat, the games we like to play, the music we like to hear, the places we love to go, the colors we like the most, the toys we like the best, the things that make us sad, the things that make us happy, and many other areas.

When you feel that students understand the concept of being unique, tell them to cut out pictures of favorite foods, activities, clothes, etc. Have them put the pictures in their envelopes. After all of the students have gathered their pictures, have them glue the pictures to their construction paper. Then, let each student share his "I Am Very Special" Collage. Or, have the student display his collage and invite classmates to guess what each picture represents. After all of the students have had a chance to share their collages, display them around the room.

No two people in the world are exactly alike. Each member of the classroom community is special and talented in his own way.

Name Card Match-Ups

This is an excellent get-to-know-you activity for the first week of school.

Supplies: two index cards for each student

Directions: Write each child's first name on an index card. To make a second set of cards, write each child's last name on an index card. (Depending on students' reading skills, you may choose to use only the first-name set of cards for this activity.) Give each student one first-name card and one last-name card. The names should not go together and should not belong to the student who receives the cards. Instruct students to walk around the room holding up the cards. They should also look for their own name cards. For example, if Mark sees that Alicia has his first-name card, he should approach her and say, "Hi, my name is Mark. What is your name?" Alicia should reply. Mark then says, "Thank you for having my card, Alicia." He then takes his first-name card and gives her the first-name card he is holding that does not belong to him. She will continue to look for the match to that card. Mark will then try to find his last-name card. When he has collected them both, he sits down.

When all of the students have found their name cards, they should take turns standing and introducing themselves to the class. Also, encourage them to add two facts, such as their favorite foods and favorite sports. So, Mark might say, "Hi, my name is Mark Adams. My favorite food is a hot dog, and my favorite sport is swimming."

Community Classroom Life Notebook

Supplies: camera; three-ring binder; one clear, plastic sheet protector for each student; one copy of the Community Member Data Sheet (page 31) for each student

Directions: Take a picture of each student. Distribute copies of the Community Member Data Sheet. Help students fill in the sheets with words or drawings, depending on their writing skills. Place each data sheet and the corresponding student's photograph back-to-back in a clear, plastic sheet protector. Place all of the pages in the three-ring binder. Keep the Community Classroom Life Notebook in a reading center or on a shelf where students can peruse the data sheets. Students love to learn about their classmates, and this project is an excellent way for them to practice reading and writing skills.

Also, if new students join the class at a later date, this is a great resource to help them get to know their new classmates. It is also useful for substitute teachers!

Community Member Data Sheet

My name is _____.

My nickname (if I have one) is _____.

I am _____ years old.

I have _____ eyes and _____ hair.

I have _____ sisters and _____ brothers.

When I am inside, my favorite thing to do is _____

_____.

When I am outside, my favorite thing to do is _____

_____.

My favorite song is _____.

I am happy when _____.

I am sad when _____.

My favorite book is _____.

What I like best about school is _____.

What I like least about school is _____.

When I grow up, I want to be _____.

INTRODUCING NEW STUDENTS

While it would be easier to have all of the students start school on the same day, this is often not the case. Many times, you will find yourself working with the group to build the foundations of a great classroom community, only to have one or more new students join the class after several days or even weeks. When this occurs, you will want to do all that you can to integrate these students into the community as quickly as possible. This chapter includes some whole-class activities that will include everyone in the process of welcoming and getting to know a new community member.

The Preview Meeting

If it is possible, try to meet with the new student and his family the day before he starts school. This will allow you to introduce yourself and the classroom to the student before the potentially overwhelming moment when he meets his classmates for the first time.

The purpose of the Preview Meeting is to:

- establish a positive relationship with both the student and the family members.

- orient the student to the classroom and a few pertinent classroom procedures.

- give the family and student any materials (papers, books, letters, etc.) that will make them feel more comfortable about the first day in a new school.

Treat this meeting like the Personal Visits (page 8) that you conducted during the summer with the other students. It is a chance for you to get acquainted with the family and start the foundation of trust that you will need throughout the year.

> Prepare the other students by encouraging them to be excited about the new community member. Remind them how important it is to accept and welcome him.

Welcome Crown

Copy one Crown Pattern (page 34) onto colorful, sturdy paper. Decorate the crown yourself or have students help you. Cut out the crown. Cut a strip of construction paper approximately 1" (2.5 cm) wide for the headband. Staple it to the ends of the crown on the Xs to make a loop that will fit the child's head. Present the new student with the crown on his first day of school. If he would like to wear it throughout the day, encourage him to do so. If not, allow him to take it home to share it with his family and keep as a memento of his first day in his new classroom community.

After the new student receives his crown, present him with a Welcome Card (page 36) or sing the Welcome Song (page 36).

Welcome Notes

If you have enough notice about a new student joining the class, help students write Welcome Notes to the new student. Make copies of the Welcome Notes (page 35) and distribute them to students. Depending on students' writing skills, you may need to help them fill in the blanks on the notes. After you help them with the writing, give them time to decorate and personalize the fronts and backs of the notes with crayons and markers. Let students present their notes to the new student when she arrives at school. Or, put them in a special bag in her cubby or on her desk for her to read when she arrives.

Crown Patterns

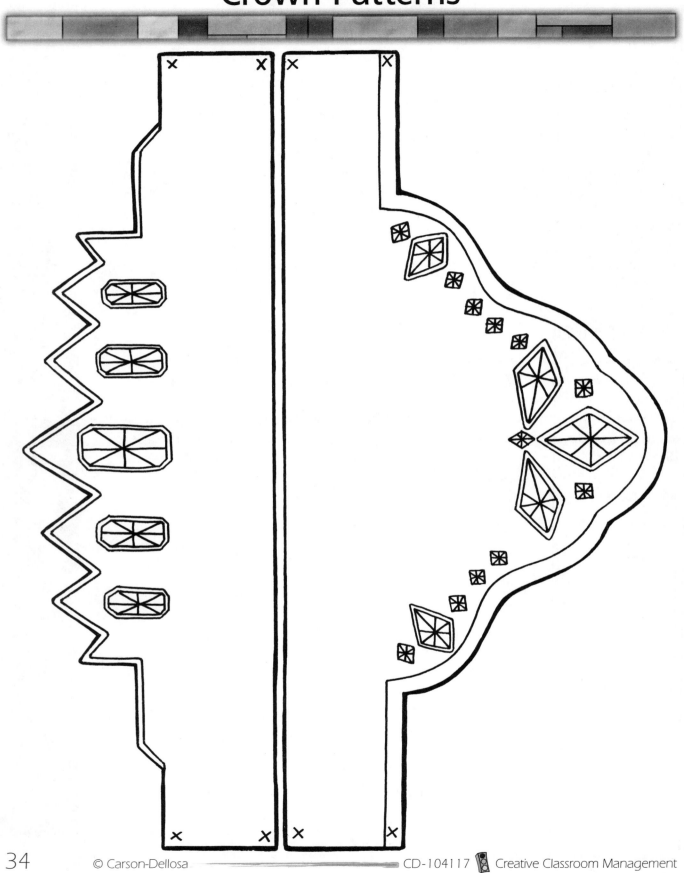

CD-104117 Creative Classroom Management

Welcome Notes

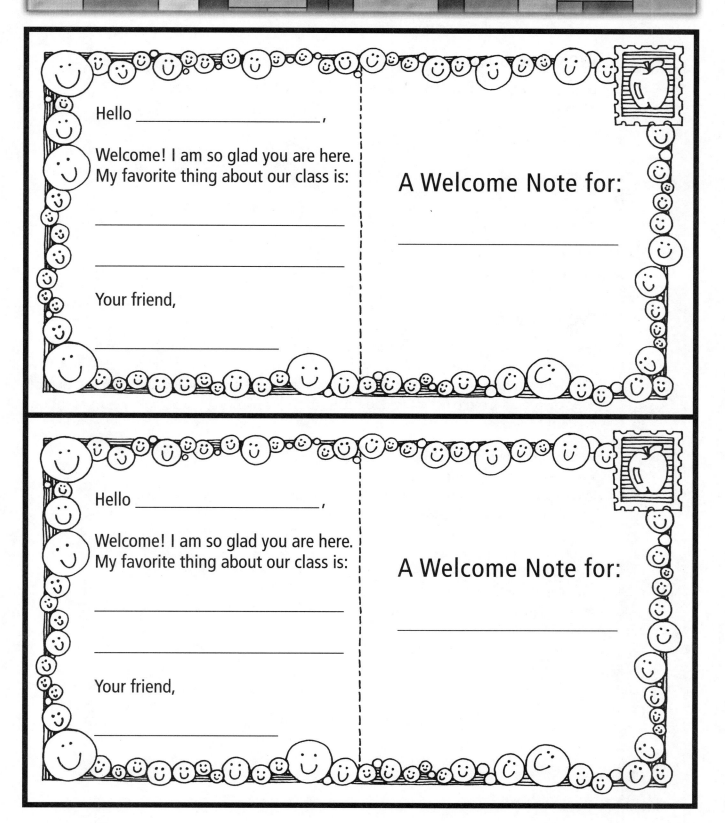

Hello _____,

Welcome! I am so glad you are here.
My favorite thing about our class is:

_____

_____

Your friend,

_____

A Welcome Note for:

_____

Hello _____,

Welcome! I am so glad you are here.
My favorite thing about our class is:

_____

_____

Your friend,

_____

A Welcome Note for:

_____

Welcome Song

Lead the class in singing the following song to welcome a new student with great enthusiasm.

(Sing to the tune of "Twinkle, Twinkle, Little Star.")

Welcome to our class today.
We can't wait till time to play.
You will be our friend indeed.
You just tell us what you need,
And we'll do our very best,
To treat you like a special guest.

Welcome Card

If you have enough notice about a new student joining the class, help students create a Welcome Card to present to the new student when she arrives. Let all of the students sign the card or draw small pictures. You can purchase a premade card, or make one of your own on a large piece of folded poster board. Following is a sample poem to include inside the card.

Welcome to our community,
We're so glad you're here.
We've so much good to share with you,
You'll want to stay all year!

If you have some questions,
Just ask, and we'll answer you.
We all belong together,
And we're glad you're here, too.

Tip for Success: When a new student first starts school, there are a variety of ways to have the class help you integrate her into the group. Following are three suggested activities. Choose one or two of them. All three could be overwhelming! Gauge your choice of activities based on your perception of the new student's personality after the Preview Meeting.

Community Helper

Select a student to act as the new student's helper. The helper should stay with the new student as much as possible throughout the day in order to offer tips and directions about procedures, schedules, and other important daily events. The helper should also include the new student in lunchtime conversations, recess games, etc., to help her feel included.

Choose a different Community Helper each day so that the new student can get to know different classmates on a one-on-one basis. If possible, meet briefly with the Community Helper each morning to give any instructions or reminders about the daily schedule that will be important for the new student to learn.

Each time students go to a special class, such as library, art, physical education, music, etc., the Community Helper will be responsible for formally introducing the new student to the teacher or administrator in that classroom. Share the following sample script with the Community Helper to demonstrate a proper introduction.

"Hello, Mrs. Anderson. This is my new friend, Clyde. This is his first day at our school. We're happy to have Clyde in our community. I am introducing him to you and some of the other members of our school community. Clyde, this is Mrs. Anderson. She is our librarian."

Mrs. Anderson would shake Clyde's hand, offer a brief welcome, and begin class. The Community Helper would then be responsible for helping Clyde learn the library procedures.

Teacher Friends

When a new child joins the class, there will be many procedures for him to learn. In a community classroom, other students can take on the role of teaching the procedures to the new student. Having different children teach the procedures helps create a real sense of responsibility for each other. It enhances their sense of community.

Instead of having just one Community Helper, you can assign several Teacher Friends. Each Teacher Friend would have a different job. For example, you might select a Library Friend to assist the new student with any library procedures or questions he may have. You might also have a Lunchtime Friend, a Behavior Plan Friend, a Reading Center Friend, or any other Friends that you think would be useful for helping a new student.

If you wish, interview students for various Teacher Friend roles. If a student is interested in being a Teacher Friend, she can approach you and describe why she thinks she would be good for the job. You can assign roles based on these interviews. Or, if you feel that students should simply be given these roles, you can make those decisions without the interviewing process.

News Reporter

Assign one to three children to interview the new student after he has been introduced to the class. They should ask the newcomer getting-to-know-you questions about some of his favorite things, his brothers and sisters, hobbies, interests, etc. Consider providing copies of a student interview sheet (page 26 or 27) for the News Reporters to use. Have the News Reporters make a formal presentation to the classroom community, sharing information from the interview.

CLASSROOM CUSTOMS

Establish a variety of classroom customs, such as a class pledge, motto, or song, to encourage a positive learning environment. Daily customs also create a sense of familiarity and comfort. Students know that the morning routine will start the same way each day. This provides a sense of security, especially for students who might have had hectic mornings at home. Daily customs are also a wonderful way to instill classroom pride. They remind students that they are part of a very special community and that their presence and cooperation are essential to the whole group.

The class will quickly memorize the customs, and you will be able to refer to them at appropriate times throughout the day. For example, when a student gets discouraged while trying to understand a concept or complete a task, you can say to her, "Now, what does our classroom motto say?" The student will respond with the motto that affirms her ability to succeed.

Classroom customs are not reserved only for the morning routine. You can use them any time that students might need encouragement or whenever you need a class cheer. Following are some suggestions for establishing your own classroom customs.

Greet Them at the Door

Even if you are still completing your own morning routine, take time to stop and stand at the door. Greet students with a big smile as they enter the room; it will mean a lot to them. Students who feel welcome and safe in their environment are much less likely to misbehave. Here are some different ways to greet them:

- Welcome them by calling them Mister or Miss. (Fill in their last names.)

- Welcome them with adjectives that begin with the same letters as their first names. "Come on in, Amazing Angela," "Nice to see you again, Terrific Tyrone," etc.

- Offer students high fives or handshakes (their choice) daily. They will appreciate this so much, and it starts the day off very well.

Tip for Success: Include "Greet Them at the Door" in your substitute teacher plans. Students will feel more comfortable with a substitute if he starts the day the same way that you do.

Class Pledge, Motto, and Song

Establish the Class Pledge, Motto, and Song as a daily routine. After students have arrived and gotten settled, ask them to stand and recite these classroom customs along with you. This is also an excellent time to share a joke, a humorous poem or riddle, or a fun, quick picture book to set a positive tone for the day.

You might choose to create the Class Pledge, Motto, and Song before the school year begins, or you may want to include students in the process. Also, consider adding movements, sounds, or gestures to animate these classroom customs.

Class Pledge

A class pledge helps students focus on the specific expectations of the class. The pledge should be brief and said in unison as part of the morning routine. It should be uplifting and spoken with joy. Reciting the pledge will help students concentrate on their daily responsibilities as members of the classroom community.

Begin by explaining that a pledge is like a promise. Discuss the concept of making a promise to the group and to yourself. Then, solicit ideas about the types of things students might do in the classroom community to make sure all of the members are happy and successful learners. If you want to involve students in the process, use these ideas to create the class pledge together. If you chose to create the pledge before school started, talk to students about the things you included. Remember that students will memorize this pledge, so it should be brief, especially for younger students. On page 41 are sample pledges that you can use or modify to suit your classroom environment. Make an enlarged copy of the Class Pledge Template (page 42). Neatly write the class pledge on the template and laminate for durability. Post in a visible place in the room.

Sample Class Pledge 1:

We are Mrs. Clark's friends.
We promise to listen carefully,
do our best work,
and treat others well.

Sample Class Pledge 2:

We are the First-Grade Friends. *(or Kindergarten Carers, Super Second Graders, etc.)*
We promise to care about each other,
help each other, and love to learn.
Our minds are the best,
and we can learn anything we want to learn.

Sample Class Pledge 3:

We are the students of Room 202.
We're bright, we're happy, and we look good, too.
We work hard each day and do our best at all times.
We promise to learn well because we have great minds.
Our classroom community is important to us.
We really care about each other, and we never fuss.

Sample Class Pledge 4:

I pledge allegiance to myself, the greatest kid around!
And, because of this, I will do my best every minute I can.
If I make a mistake, I will learn from it,
forgive myself, and move on.
I am a neat kid and a smart worker.
I am lovable. I am capable. And, I'm glad I'm ME!

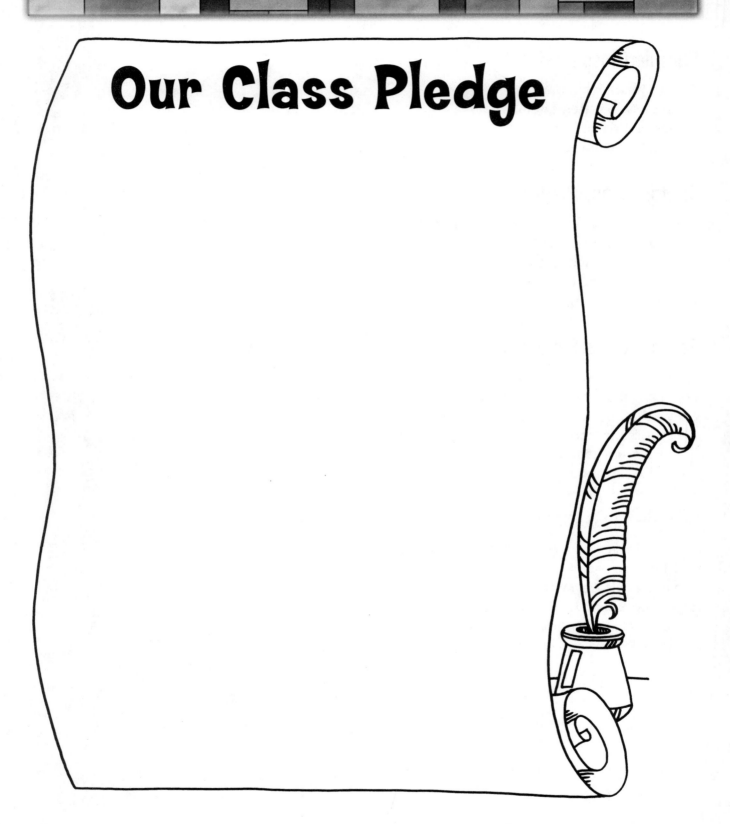

Our Class Pledge

Class Motto

A motto is a brief phrase or sentence used to express a principle. A class motto should be used throughout the day whenever students are feeling frustrated and need to positively refocus their energy. When students are facing what they believe to be tough situations in class, ask them to recite the class motto. Following are some sample mottoes that you can use or modify to suit your classroom environment. Make an enlarged copy of the Class Motto Template (page 45). Neatly write the class motto on the template and laminate for durability. Post in a visible place in the room.

Sample Class Mottoes:

We can do it because we're great and we're smart.

We're above all of the rest because we always give our best.

We're phenomenal learners. We're the cream of the crop!

Tip for Success: Don't be afraid to use a "big word" like *phenomenal*. Teach the word to students, and they will take pride in being able to say and use it correctly. Tell them to share the motto with their families. They love to "show off" their new skills, and their families will be proud of them for learning advanced vocabulary.

Class Song

Songs are especially useful teaching tools for young students. Songs make it easier for children to memorize content. Creating a class song is easy. Choose a popular tune that you and the children already know. Write the class song using the tune but change the words. The song should talk about students as a class and make them feel special.

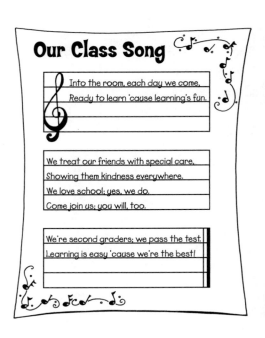

On page 44 are sample songs that you can use or modify to suit your classroom environment. Make an enlarged copy of the Class Song Template (page 46). Neatly write the words of the class song on the lines of the template. Laminate for durability. Post in a visible place in the room.

Sample Class Song 1:

(Sing to the tune of "Mary Had a Little Lamb.")

Every day I come to school,
Just to learn, and see you.   *(Point to classmates.)*
Learning is so fun for me;
I do it every day!

Sample Class Song 2:

(Sing to the tune of "She'll Be Comin' Round the Mountain.")

We learn great new things every day; we're smart!
We treat others with kindness from our hearts.
We are followin' directions.
So we will not need corrections.
We love learning every day because we're smart! *(Shout, "Yee-haw!" and jump in the air.)*

Sample Class Song 3:

(Sing to the tune of "Up on the Housetop.")

Into the room, each day we come,
Ready to learn 'cause learning's fun.
We treat our friends with special care,
Showing them kindness everywhere.
We love school; yes, we do.
Come join us; you will, too.
We're second graders; we pass the test.
Learning is easy 'cause we're the best!

Our Class Motto

Other Classroom Songs

As the year progresses, add other useful songs to your collection. Singing is an excellent learning and classroom management tool. Some children respond to a song better than they respond to a spoken request. You may want to regularly sing directions to students. Any set of notes will do. The lyrical sound of your voice will often capture their attention and stick with them so that they remember the instructions better. If you don't believe you sing well, don't worry about it. Students love to sing and hear their teachers sing! Following are useful songs for controlling situations that can be chaotic, such as lining up, transitioning to a new lesson, and finding seats and sitting still. The songs can be sung or chanted in a singsongy voice. There aren't specific tunes to follow; just make sure you use the same tune every time you sing each song so that students recognize it immediately and know how to respond.

Are We Ready? Song

The "Are We Ready? Song" is used before the class enters the hallway to walk to another classroom, the playground, or the lunchroom.

Teacher: "Are we ready?" *Students:* "Yes, we're ready!"
Teacher: "Are your eyes on me?" *Students:* "Yes, they are."
Teacher: "Are your hands by your sides?" *Students:* "Yes, they are."
Teacher: "Are your mouths quiet?" *Students: (silence)*
Teacher: "Then, we're ready!"

Open-Shut Them Song

The "Open-Shut Them Song" is used when it is time for students to find seats and sit still. It is especially useful when transitioning to carpet time or any time when students are changing seats.

Open, shut them; open, shut them. *(Open fingers wide, clasp hands together; repeat.)*
Give a little clap. *(Clap softly three times.)*
Open, shut them; open, shut them. *(Open fingers wide, clasp hands together; repeat.)*
Place them in your lap. *(Sit tall and place clasped hands in laps.)*

Give Me Five Song

This song is simply one line. It is used to get students' attention after a transition or during a particularly rowdy moment.

Teacher: "Give me five."

After you sing, "Give me five," students should respond by sitting still and holding up five fingers to show you that they have completed the five steps:

1. Eyes are on speaker.
2. Body is still.
3. Hands are free and still.
4. Mouth is quiet.
5. Ears are listening.

Any time you say or sing, "Give me five," students should stop what they are doing and "give you five." If they do not comply, practice using the "Give Me Five Song" with them again and discuss its meaning and importance. Since this is the signal for students to give you their undivided attention, they must know and use it promptly and accurately.

Class Attention Song

The "Class Attention Song" is a variation of the "Give Me Five Song." It is also used to get students' attention after a transition or during a particularly rowdy moment. If students do not respond immediately after you sing, "Eyes on me," repeat the first two lines with an assertive, yet calm, voice. If some students are still not looking at you, calmly and firmly ask them to comply. You may even choose to do this in the same singsongy voice as the song. For example, "Mark, Lisa, and Shanice, thank you for putting your eyes on me." When you have compliance, move on to the third line.

Teacher: "One, two, three,
   Eyes on me."
   (pause)
   "Give me five."

Circle Time

Before the first circle time of the school year, create a Brag Bag. This should be a large gift bag or canvas bag. Write a sentence starter for each child on a sentence strip. For example, you might write, *Jon is proud of himself because* _____ , *Abigail is proud of herself because* _____ , etc. Make sure you have one sentence strip for each member of the class. Place all of the strips inside the Brag Bag. You will use the Brag Bag throughout the year during circle time, so keep it in a convenient place.

Once a week, invite students to join you for circle time. Have students sit with you on the floor in a circle. Begin circle time by singing a favorite song or sharing a short story. Then, bring out the Brag Bag. Reach into the Brag Bag, select a sentence strip, and read the sentence starter. Explain that students should raise their hands if they can think of things that the selected student should be proud of. For example, one classmate might think that Abigail should be proud that she learned to tie her shoes, another might think that she should be proud that she lost her first tooth, etc. When several students have offered suggestions, have Abigail select the one she is most proud of or let her choose an idea of her own. You should then help her fill in the blank on her sentence strip. Post the strip on a "brag board" or send it home for her to share with her family. Depending on how much time you have, try to complete two or three Brag Bag sentence strips during each meeting of circle time.

Variations:

- Circle time can also be used to read and discuss stories about important character traits, such as integrity, compassion, self-discipline, perseverance, fairness, courage, etc. Discuss the stories with students after you finish reading to make sure they understand why it is important to have good character in a caring classroom community.

- Celebrate birthdays during circle time. Let the birthday child wear a special birthday crown. (Use the Crown Patterns on page 34. Assembly instructions are found on page 33.) Then, have each person in the circle, beginning with yourself, complete the following sentence, "_____ , you are special because _____ ." Remember to set aside a special celebration day for each student whose birthday occurs when school is not in session.

PROCEDURES

The previous chapters of this book outline activities for beginning to establish a sense of community in the classroom. They help students get to know each other and celebrate their similarities and differences while building a sense of mutual respect. These activities are just one part of creating a classroom community. In this chapter, you will find guidelines for establishing classroom procedures. A sense of community can only be developed in an atmosphere of order. For this reason, it is important to clearly define what is acceptable behavior and how you expect students to conduct themselves in certain situations.

It is your responsibility as a teacher to show students how they are expected to behave and set a clear plan that they understand. Even if some children have a learned habit of misbehaving, they can be taught a better way to manage their behavior. Some students misbehave because they have not been taught what is expected of them in all situations. You might assume that they should know the expectations. Sometimes, this simply is not the case. Even children who are not prone to misbehaving may sometimes act in a way that does not follow your expectations because they have learned to do the task in a different way. In this case, their behavior is not necessarily wrong, but it is still disruptive to the classroom plan. If you establish and teach classroom procedures from the beginning of the year, there will be no need for confusion or frustration.

Begin by letting go of the assumption that children already know what is expected of them. Teach them what is expected in the classroom community. Explain that even though they might do some of these things differently at home, they will need to follow the procedures for the whole class to be happy and successful. Take the time to teach the procedures at the beginning of the year. While it is time consuming, it will save you time throughout the year because students will understand what is expected of them and require less correction.

> A sense of community can only be developed in an atmosphere of order. It is important to clearly define what is acceptable behavior and how you expect students to conduct themselves in certain situations.

Preparing the Procedures

The successful design and utilization of the procedures will play a major role in classroom community management. Many behavior problems exist because students do not follow directions. Often, the reason students do not follow directions is that they have one interpretation of the directions, and you have another. Teaching procedures eliminates any unclear expectations. It allows you to be certain that a student who disobeys has made that choice and has not simply been unclear about what was expected.

What is a procedure? A procedure is a specific method or process for how a task should be accomplished within the classroom community. It includes What, Where, When, and How information. For everything you want students to do in a certain way, particularly something that is done on a regular basis, you should have a procedure.

Procedures prepare you for handling misbehavior. If there is a procedure in place and a student chooses not to follow it, you have a script for addressing the situation. For example, if Sarah does not raise her hand to ask a question, you can simply say, "Sarah, what is the procedure for asking a question in our community?" Then, you can handle the situation based on her response and the established behavior plan. Without a procedure, you might become frustrated, raise your voice, or use other, less effective behavior management techniques.

> For everything you want students to do in a certain way, particularly something that is done on a regular basis, you should have a procedure.

Creating Procedures

Before school starts, make a list of activities that will require procedures. These are things that students will do often, and they are also things that you want them to do in specific ways. Think about the behavior that you expect during these times. Remember that procedures are only for activities that will always be done the same way. There are some activities that are too specific and do not require procedures because they are unique occurrences, such as visiting a book fair. However, a procedure for visiting other classrooms would probably cover the behavior you expect when students go to a book fair. Use the Procedure Planning Worksheet (page 53) to list when you will need procedures. If you forget a procedure or realize later in the year that you want to add a new procedure, feel free! You are not limited to the procedures that you have when you begin the school year. But, preparing in advance will be a helpful time-saver in the long run. Following are some potential times when a procedure might be useful.

- Entering the classroom
- During a fire drill
- Asking a question
- During free time
- During "carpet time"
- Eating lunch
- Having indoor recess
- Lining up
- Feeding the class pet

- Preparing for dismissal
- During snack time
- During group work
- Working in a center
- Requesting to use the rest room
- Turning in homework
- Having outside recess
- Going to other classrooms
- Playing with the class pet

Remember, you can add new procedures as the need arises throughout the year. But, the more prepared you are from day one, the better!

Procedure Planning Worksheet

1. Think about the daily routine in the classroom. List any activities that students should do in a certain way each day, such as entering the classroom, putting away their belongings, completing morning work, preparing for lunch, getting out supplies for the next subject, etc.

   _____

   _____

2. Are there any regular variations in the daily schedule, such as art, music, physical education, library, etc? List any procedures that you will need during these activities.

   _____

   _____

3. Are there any activities during group time that will require procedures, such as asking a question, requesting to use the rest room, sharpening pencils, working with others, etc.? List them here.

   _____

   _____

4. Are there any activities during independent time that will require procedures, such as handling books in the reading center, using classroom games and toys, using the computer, etc.? List them here.

   _____

   _____

5. Are there any general behavior requirements that will need procedures, such as the "Give Me Five Song," lining up to leave the room, gathering for story time, keeping personal areas neat, etc.? List them here.

   _____

   _____

6. Can you think of any other classroom activities that will require procedures? List them here.

   _____

   _____

Writing Procedures

When you have completed your list, you will need to write procedures. You may be thinking that writing procedures sounds like a great idea, but where do you begin? First, remember to make them your own. You may have school rules to consider. Or, you might use certain vocabulary, such as *inside voices* instead of *low voices*. You might also use songs as part of your procedures. (See the sample Nap Time procedure on page 57.) Use the steps and techniques that work in your particular setting.

Remember, there should be no more than five steps in a procedure and preferably only three or four. Each step should include only one instruction. Rather than, "Step 1: Clear your desk and put away your book bag," you should write, "Step 1: Clear your desk. Step 2: Put away your book bag."

When you write the steps of the procedures, use specific, definitive statements. For example, "Be nice" is not an appropriate step because you leave room for interpreting the word *nice*. Instead, use a definitive statement, such as, "Keep hands, feet, and objects to yourself." In effect, you are instructing students to "be nice," but you are also telling them exactly how you expect them to be nice.

As you write, you will find that you repeat yourself. That is OK. Many procedures will include instructions, such as "Remain seated," "Eyes on your own work," or "Wait until the teacher calls on you." Continue to be this specific. This straightforward presentation of your expectations will be beneficial for you and students. They will know exactly what is expected of them, and if they choose to misbehave, they will know exactly where they went wrong.

In order to keep procedures to three to five steps, you will find yourself embedding procedures within other procedures. This is OK, too! It shows students that many activities depend on other activities. For instance, if you have a Lunchtime procedure, one of the steps might be "Wash hands." You do not need to explain this further within the Lunchtime procedure because you already have a separate Washing Hands procedure.

You will also find that several procedures naturally follow others. For example, you might have a Lining Up procedure and an In the Hallway procedure. The first step of the In the Hallway procedure is not to line up because that was already addressed in the Lining Up procedure. If you find yourself writing a procedure with more than five steps, look to see if you are actually combining two procedures into one. Split it into two separate procedures, and you should be able to write three to five steps for each.

Remember, a Good Procedure Includes:

1. the name of the procedure
2. three to five specific directions that you want students to follow when completing the procedure
3. directions that address what materials are needed, where students are expected to be, and the desired noise level

For example, the procedure for Snack Time might be:

Snack Time

1. Clear your desk.
2. Bring your snack to your seat.
3. Use a low voice when talking.
4. Clean your area when finished.

Of course, you might choose to modify these instructions depending on various factors that apply to the classroom needs. This sample names the procedure, gives three to five specific directions, and addresses what materials are needed, where students should be, and the acceptable noise level.

Check the procedures using the What, Where, When, and How test.

1. Does the procedure tell *what* they need?
2. Does the procedure tell *where* they are expected to be?
3. Does the procedure tell *when* they will use this procedure?
4. Does the procedure tell *how* to complete the procedure?

Let's check the Snack Time example.

1. Does the procedure tell *what* they need?
   Yes. They need clean desks and their snacks.
2. Does the procedure tell *where* they are expected to be?
   Yes. They should be in their seats.
3. Does the procedure tell *when* they will use this procedure?
   Yes. They will use the procedure during Snack Time.
4. Does the procedure tell *how* to complete the procedure?
   Yes. The steps are clear and brief, and they tell students how to have a successful Snack Time in the classroom.

Sample Procedures

Following are some sample procedures to give you a starting point.

Entering the Classroom

1. Walk into the room.
2. Put away your belongings.
3. Quietly take your seat.
4. Use a low voice when talking.

Lining Up

1. Walk to the door.
2. Keep hands, feet, and objects to yourself.
3. Form a single-file line.
4. No voices.

In the Hallway

1. Keep hands, feet, and objects to yourself.
2. Walk.
3. Stay in line.
4. No voices.

Independent Work

1. Sit in your seat.
2. Keep your eyes on your own work.
3. Raise your hand if you need help.
4. No voices.

Group Work

1. Take turns.
2. Listen to each other.
3. Work together.
4. Use a low voice.

Asking a Question

1. Raise your hand.
2. Remain seated.
3. Wait to be recognized.
4. No voices until recognized.

Nap Time

1. When you hear the Nap Time song, get your nap mat.
2. Place your mat on the floor.
3. Lie still and rest.
4. No voices.

Feeding the Fish

1. Wash your hands.
2. Remove a small pinch of food from the food can.
3. Close the food can.
4. Sprinkle the food in the water.
5. Wash your hands.

Fire Drill

1. Line up quickly without running.
2. Follow your teacher to the safety area.
3. Follow directions from adults in charge.
4. No voices.

You may also choose to post reminders about ideas that appear in the procedures. For example:

Voices in the Classroom

Whispers Only should ONLY be heard by the person next to you.
Low Voices should only be heard by two people next to you.
Inside Voices should be used when your group needs to hear you.
Outside Voices may be heard by several people around you.
No Voices or *Be Quiet* means NO voices should be heard at all.

Making Procedure Cards

After you have written the procedures, you will need to make one card for each procedure. You can use 8½" × 11" (21.5 cm × 28 cm) card stock, poster board, or regular paper. If you use paper, consider laminating each piece for durability.

Print neatly on the cards or use a computer. Use a large font so that students can read it when you hold it up in front of the class. At the top, list the name of the procedure. Then, write the specific steps of the procedure.

For younger students who may still be learning to read, consider adding clip art or simple illustrations to help them understand the procedure cards. Use the illustration below as an example.

Collect the cards in a three-ring binder for easy storage. It is helpful to organize the binder. For example, you might arrange the cards by group activities, individual activities, and outside the classroom activities. Consider printing the cards for each section on a different color to make it easy to arrange them. Keep the binder in an accessible location so that you can refer to it as needed throughout the year. It is also helpful to have the binder available for family members to browse when they visit the classroom. Then, they will know what is expected of each student and will be able to support the procedures, as well.

Independent Work

1. Sit in your seat.

2. Keep your eyes on your own work.

3. Raise your hand if you need help.

4. No voices.

Feeding the Fish

1. Wash your hands.

2. Remove a small pinch of food from the food can.

3. Close the food can.

4. Sprinkle the food in the water.

5. Wash your hands.

Teaching the Procedures

You must teach the procedures to students. Never assume they understand what you mean when you say, "Get ready for _____ ." These words mean different things to different people. For example, if you say, "Get ready for Snack Time," without first teaching the procedure, one student may take his snack and sit on the floor because that is what he does at home when he has a snack. He may not be misbehaving intentionally; he just does not know how you expect him to complete that particular activity because you have not taught him. You must teach students what you expect from them. To teach a procedure, you should demonstrate it and have students practice what you have demonstrated.

When teaching a procedure, follow these steps:

1. Display the procedure card.
2. Review the steps by reading the card. Demonstrate the steps as you reread them. Then, read them again. If students are old enough, have them read the steps with you the third time.
3. Question students for understanding while you demonstrate each step.
4. Practice the procedure with students.

Procedures should be taught just before you need them. Do not teach the entire book of procedures as soon as students are in their seats on the first day of school. Not only will they be intimidated by the process, but they will forget most of the information because they will not be able to immediately apply it. So, 10 minutes before going to music class for the first time, teach the procedure for Going to Other Classrooms. Then, when you walk to music for the first time, students will remember the procedure they just learned because they have practiced it and received reinforcing praise from you.

Remember to be patient the first few weeks of school. You will teach procedures daily during this time. You will also need to review procedures after a break from school, perhaps at the beginning of each new quarter, and any other time when it seems that students need a reminder to get back on track. While this may seem time consuming, especially at the beginning of the school year, the order that it will bring to your classroom experience will be well worth it.

Sample: Teaching a Procedure

Refer to the Snack Time procedure (page 55). When it is time for snack on the first day of school, you will need to teach the procedure.

First, hold up the procedure card.

Then, read all of the steps slowly.

Next, read each step again and demonstrate the step as you read it. Question students for understanding during this process. Ask several questions after each step to ensure that students fully understand the importance of following the procedure. This will also help to eliminate those "But, why do we have to . . . ?" questions that some students are inclined to ask.

1. *Clear your desk.* (Remove any items from the student desk where you are seated and put them away.) Question for understanding by asking questions, such as, "Meghan, is it OK for me to throw my books in my desk and jam my pencil in my cubby?" If you select one student to answer the question, the process will remain much calmer.

2. *Bring your snack to your seat.* (Go quietly and calmly to the cubby area and retrieve your snack. Bring it to the desk where you were seated and prepare to eat it.) Question for understanding: "Grant, is it acceptable for me to run as fast as I can to my cubby to get my snack because I'm really hungry and so excited that it's time to eat?" Seek appropriate answers from students.

3. *Use a low voice.* (Chat quietly with students seated near you.) Question for understanding: "Maria, why do you think we should use low voices during Snack Time?" Seek appropriate answers from students.

4. *Clean your area when finished.* (Dispose of any trash and clean the desk surface.) Question for understanding: "Xavier, is it OK to put my apple core in my desk and wipe off the top of the desk with my sleeve?" Seek appropriate answers from students. It is fun to use silly questions like this with students. It will make them laugh while still reminding them that inappropriate behavior is not acceptable.

 Creative Classroom Management

Finally, practice the procedure with students. Have them pretend it is Snack Time and follow each step. Read the steps aloud and have them perform each step. Offer reinforcing praise as they do each step correctly and provide any words of instruction as needed.

Presenting and practicing each procedure in this manner clearly establishes your expectations for the activity. Use this method to teach each procedure. Remember, always teach a procedure just before students need to use it. If you try to teach too many procedures at once, students will be overwhelmed, and the time will essentially be wasted. Use the Procedure Checklist on page 62 to make sure that you have properly taught each procedure.

The first few weeks of school will be spent emphasizing the procedures. Teach them again and again. Have students practice them again and again until they automatically know what is expected when you say, "Get ready for _____."

> **Always teach a procedure just before students need to use it. If you try to teach too many procedures at once, students will be overwhelmed!**

Procedure Checklist

Ensure that students know the procedures!

Make sure you have completed the following seven steps each time you teach a procedure.

Did you . . .

1. _____ hold the procedure card in a position that allowed each student to clearly see it from where he was sitting?

2. _____ read each step of the procedure clearly and explain any part that could be misinterpreted?

3. _____ demonstrate each step of the procedure as you read it?

4. _____ have students read the card along with you?

5. _____ question students for understanding?

6. _____ have students practice the procedure before actually using it?

7. _____ offer students praise or clarification for how accurately they followed the procedure?

CD-104117 Creative Classroom Management

THE BEHAVIOR PLAN

It is critical that you are consistent with discipline and the administration of the behavior plan. Again, if students know what to expect from you, they will be more comfortable and confident in their environment. They like a sense of order. A plan is crucial to the success of a classroom. Providing a written plan helps ensure consistency.

Just like the procedures discussed earlier, you must teach the behavior plan through modeling. Students need to practice the plan, and you need to question for understanding to make sure that students know what is expected of them. Teaching the behavior plan should be part of the schedule for the first week of school, even before you begin to teach the procedures. Many procedures are based on the classroom rules that are included in the behavior plan. Rules are rules; procedures are directions for specific activities. Students must understand the rules before they learn the procedures.

Creating a Behavior Plan

Before school begins, write your behavior plan. It will consist of rules (or community agreements), positives, and consequences. You might choose to wait until school starts to finalize the positives because you can poll students and have them help you compose this list. If they have a hand in deciding the rewards they would like to receive, they are much more likely to comply with the rules. If you teach especially young students, it might be too difficult to make the list together. Decide what you want to do based on the students you teach.

> Be consistent with discipline and the administration of the behavior plan. If students know what to expect from you, they will be more comfortable and confident in their environment.

Community Agreements: The Rules

First, select three to four agreements for the class. The rules are different from procedures because they apply at all times. Students should always follow these rules. They should be simple, brief, and easily understood so that students can memorize them. It is hard for young children to memorize more than three or four rules, and memorizing the rules is imperative.

Following is a sample list of rules:

Mr. Vanelli's Classroom Community Agreements

1. Follow directions.
2. Keep hands, feet, and objects to yourself.
3. Do not call people names or use bad words.

As you can see, these rules are broad, and they cover a variety of situations. They almost always apply to any classroom situation. Rule number one is especially important because it is so general. Any time a student is not doing what you ask, he is breaking rule number one.

When you teach the behavior plan on the first day of school, begin by questioning students about the meaning of the words *agreement* and *rule*. For example, ask them, "What do you think an agreement is?" (Accept appropriate answers.) Lead them to the idea that an agreement is very much like a promise.

Some other leading questions for the discussion might include:

"What are some things we should do to make this community run smoothly?"

"What agreements or promises might we want to have?"

"What are some things we should agree upon so that we can all feel good in our classroom?"

"What will help us learn to trust each other?"

Ask for students' thoughts and ideas and write them on the board. Have them share why they think it is important to have rules. After students have demonstrated an understanding of the concept of a rule, teach and model the classroom community rules using the strategy that is outlined in the Procedures chapter (page 59).

Rewards for Compliance: Positives

Having established and taught the agreements, it is important to have positives that students will receive as a result of their compliance. Even if you choose to seek student input for this list, you should have a planned list of suggestions before school starts. Plan to include three to five positives on your list. It might include:

- Compliments from you or classmates

- Positive signals (thumbs-up, big smile, or high five)

- Notes and phone calls home

- Certificates sent home

- Prizes (donated by parents or purchased at a discount store)

- Privileges (sit at teacher's desk for 10 minutes, line leader, teacher's helper, etc.)

- "No homework" passes

- Tickets (See page 83.)

- Good behavior badges to wear all day

If you choose to have students help you compose the list, talk to them about positive rewards for good behavior. For example, "Raise your hand if you can tell me something that makes you feel good when you are around a friend." Lead students to offer answers, such as a smile and a compliment. Write their suggested positives on the board. Also, ask students about ways that you can tell their families about the great job that they are doing in the classroom community. Remember to use these positives regularly to reinforce positive behavior by individuals, small groups, or the entire class.

Choosing to Misbehave: Consequences

Finally, make a list of consequences that will be enforced if students choose not to follow the agreements. The consequences should be a hierarchy, with the first consequence applying to the first violation, the second consequence to the second violation, etc. In some cases of severe misbehavior, you will jump straight to the last consequence—usually a visit to the principal's office. But, most often, you will follow the hierarchy because it is consistent and students know what to expect.

Establish consequences that are disliked but not harmful. Remember, a consequence is intended to give students a chance to regroup, rethink their actions, and make better choices in the future. The consequences should be easy to deliver without a great deal of interruption. Do not think of consequences as punishment. Punishment often makes students angrier, and that can escalate the problem.

When the list is established, you will teach it to students through modeling and questioning, the same way you taught the other two sections of the classroom behavior plan. Talk with students about what happens if a community member chooses to break the rules. Remember to use the word *choose* repeatedly. Make sure students understand that it is not your fault when they receive consequences because they chose to misbehave and, therefore, chose to receive consequences. Also, talk with them about how it affects other students when someone breaks the rules. Discuss the classroom disruptions, hurt feelings, and other results of misbehavior. Lead students to talk about how it hurts the community when one or more students are not on task.

Following is a sample list of consequences:

1. Verbal redirect
2. Time out
3. Miss five minutes of recess
4. Phone call home
5. Visit to principal's office

Severe disruption: Go directly to principal's office.

Verbal Redirect

A verbal redirect occurs when you call a student's name and give a direction to correct the misbehavior, such as, "Micah, sit down and start your worksheet. No voices." You might use this step more than once before moving to the next consequence. When you give a second verbal redirect, mention the next consequence. "Micah, if you do not sit down and start your worksheet as I asked you to do, you will choose to go to time out."

Time Out

A time out can be scheduled for a certain number of minutes that is posted on the consequences list (an appropriate time for students' age level), or it can be determined on a case-by-case basis. Determine an area of the room where the misbehaving student will sit quietly during the time away from the rest of the class. She should sit and think about her misbehavior but not participate in classroom activities. If you use a set amount of time, do not forget to watch the clock so that the student will know when she can return to the classroom community. Consider using a timer as a reminder.

Note: If a student finds herself in time out more than once during the day, do not increase the number of minutes that she is there. Remain consistent. If the consequence states that time out is for five minutes, then time out should always be five minutes long.

You can also use the time out consequence as a brief correction. For example, "Corey, go to the time out chair. You may return to your desk as soon as you commit to keeping your hands to yourself as it says in our agreements."

If you do not like the term *time out*, give it a name that is useful for students, such as *thinking time*.

Miss Five Minutes of Recess

When the class goes outside for recess, have the student who is being disciplined stand or sit beside you for the first five minutes. (This should be lowered to three minutes for kindergarten students.) Students do not like watching their friends playing without them. This is a very brief and effective consequence. It is more effective than missing the entire recess because that tends to anger the student rather than serve as a reminder.

Phone Call Home

After a student has received the first three consequences on the list, it is time to talk to a family member about the behavior problems. Make a list of infractions so that you can speak specifically about the student's disruptions. When you are calm and have a few minutes alone to make the call, contact the family member. First, share one or two positive things about the student. Never start with a negative! Then, express your concern about the student's behavior. Never express anger. For example, "Robert is a terrific thinker and offers great ideas in class. Lately, however, he has been yelling out his thoughts or questions during our seat work time. This is disturbing to his classmates' learning and stops him from receiving the help he needs. In our classroom, students should raise their hands and wait to be called on if they wish to answer or ask a question. Robert is a fine young man with a great eagerness for learning. I would like for you to speak with him about the importance of raising his hand before he speaks."

Then, affirm or clarify the family member's comments and thank him or her for taking time to talk with you about the student. Remind the family member that Robert is very important to you and tell the family member that you will be contacting him or her within a few days with a progress report. End the phone call by summarizing what he or she has committed to do and what you will do to help Robert comply. Thank the family member again and reassure him or her of your confidence in Robert.

Visit to Principal's Office

This consequence is reserved for major infractions of the rules or repeated misbehavior. Students do not like to go to the principal's office, so you should not often have to use this consequence.

Some Other Suggested Consequences

The five consequences just described are often very effective with young students. Following are some other useful suggestions.

Note Home to Family

Have the student write a letter to his family telling them what happened and how he will behave differently in the future. Ask family members to sign and return the letter to you the next day so that you will know they saw it.

Write or Draw in a Behavior Journal

Provide a behavior journal or a worksheet with questions and prompts that will lead students to write about their misbehavior. Young students can also draw pictures. The words or pictures should demonstrate what students did wrong, as well as what they should have done instead. Be sure to talk with students about the incidents before you send them to rejoin the rest of the class. Students should clearly understand what behavior was wrong and the proper way to act in the future.

Last in Line for Lunch or Recess

Young students really do not like this consequence. It is brief but effective.

Miss Five Minutes of Free Time

During a time when the class is completing a fun activity, have a child who has misbehaved sit in a chair in the back of the room where she can see her classmates but cannot participate. Once again, be sure to talk with the child about her behavior and what she learned during her time alone before she returns to class.

Go to a Buddy Room

Make an agreement with a teacher who teaches students one grade older or one grade younger than you do. (This will not work with a teacher who teaches the same grade that you do.) Provide that teacher with a box of worksheets or behavior journals and pencils for your students. When necessary, send a misbehaving student to that teacher's classroom for a 10-minute time out. While in the room, that student should sit quietly in a time out area and work on the materials you provided. He is not allowed to join in the class's routine. This is especially effective for students who try to be "class clowns" and gain audiences when they are in time out in their own classrooms. When you remove them from their usual audiences, they have no choice but to think about their behavior and how to modify it.

When the other teacher sends the student back to your classroom, remember to talk with him and process the new goal for positive behavior, express your trust in his ability, and return to regular classroom procedure.

If the student misbehaves while in the buddy room, he must go to the principal's office.

The Classroom Community Behavior Plan

When you have composed all three parts of the behavior plan, write them on a large piece of poster board and display it prominently in the classroom. Leave room at the bottom of the poster for students to sign their names to show that they agree to abide by the Classroom Community Behavior Plan. Remind students that their signatures are symbols of their promise to keep the agreements. Laminate the poster after all students have signed it and display it for the entire school year. Also, send home a letter that describes the plan. (A sample letter is on page 72.) Ask families to review the plan with students and sign and return it the next day. This will ensure that you and the families are working together, and it will inform them from the first days of school about your plan and the way that you will conduct the classroom.

Tip for Success: Provide an incentive for returning the signed letter. Place all of the signed letters in a drawing for a prize, such as a gift certificate for two to the movies.

Working with Families

- Remember to specifically document all problems with students. It is important to keep these records in your student files so that you have specific examples when you speak to families.

- Be prompt. At the first sign of a problem, contact families. Do not wait until issues have piled up. They can become upset if they feel they have been left out of what is going on. They also might be able to help you with issues if you contact them early. Give them a chance to be as involved as possible.

- Remember to communicate appropriately through words and gestures that show your belief in the fact that together you and the family can resolve the issue.

- When you are not sure about how to handle a problem, seek administrative assistance. The administration can serve as a good guide or mediator when handling difficult situations.

Sample Behavior Plan Display

Mrs. Fox's Classroom Community Behavior Plan

Class Rules:

1. Follow directions.
2. Keep hands, feet, and objects to yourself.
3. Do not call people names or use bad words.

Positives:

1. Compliments
2. Positive signals
3. Notes and phone calls home
4. Prizes or privileges

Consequences:

1. Verbal redirect
2. Time out
3. Miss five minutes of recess
4. Phone call home
5. Visit to principal's office

Severe disruption: Go directly to principal's office.

Jennifer   Rick   Nicole   Jeremy

Steven   Mario   Dawn

Logan   TAYLOR   Carol

Sample Behavior Plan Letter

Dear Families,

I am so excited about this school year! We have so many wonderful things planned. In order for all of the students in our classroom community to have the best possible learning experience, I have developed a Classroom Community Behavior Plan. It clearly outlines the community rules, as well as the positive rewards for good behavior and the consequences for poor behavior choices. This plan will allow me to guide your children in making good decisions about their behavior.

My goal is for all students to experience a positive educational climate and extraordinary academic growth. I know you share my goal, and I look forward to working with you for a successful school year.

Please discuss the plan with your child. Then, sign, detach, and return the bottom portion to me tomorrow. I look forward to a fantastic school year!

Sincerely,

_____

Our Classroom Community Behavior Plan

Class Rules:

1. Follow directions.
2. Keep hands, feet, and objects to yourself.
3. Do not call people names or use bad words.

Positives:

1. Compliments
2. Positive signals
3. Notes and phone calls home
4. Prizes or privileges

Consequences:

1. Verbal redirect
2. Time out
3. Miss five minutes of recess
4. Phone call home
5. Visit to principal's office

Severe disruption: Go directly to principal's office.

- -

I have read the Classroom Community Behavior Plan and discussed it

with my child, _____ .

_____   _____
Signature   Date

Comments: _____

CD-104117 Creative Classroom Management

Delivering the Consequences

Now that everyone is onboard with your behavior plan, how do you administer the consequences? First, consequences should always be delivered in a calm, matter-of-fact manner. Avoid sarcasm or a judgmental tone. Never deliver a consequence with an angry voice or look. You should always deliver consequences as soon as possible after the misbehavior and in a consistent manner. Even if you have a headache, you must still be consistent and not overreact or ignore the behavior because you don't feel well. Consistency is very important to students.

Most importantly, remember to use a "forgive and forget" attitude. Always judge the behavior, not the students. When the consequence has been delivered and served, move on. Be ready to provide a clean slate each new day.

Firmly and clearly tell the student what you expect. "I expect you to circle the correct picture in your workbook." Make eye contact. Do not point your finger in a child's face. This will feel like a demeaning punishment. Use nonverbal communication to add nonthreatening emphasis to your words. Your gestures should show that you are administering consequences because you care, not because you are angry.

Provide students with consequences every time they are disruptive or off task.

Be prompt. The consequence should be carried out as soon as possible after the student misbehaves. If you are making a phone call home, do it the same day the student is disruptive. Do not wait until the third or fourth time the child repeats the behavior. Families want to know what is happening with their children before misbehaviors become repeated problems. Even if it seems like families are not interested or you are getting no response, do not stop informing them of students' behavior.

Remember to contact families when behavior improves. It is important to let them know when things are going well! This is especially important for students who misbehave often.

Tracking Behavior

When you have implemented a behavior plan, it is important to create a visual display for young students. In addition to the posted behavior plan (pages 70–71), you will need a tracking chart. This lets students know where they stand at all times. The chart should be placed in the back of the classroom so that it is not viewed as a tool for embarrassing students who misbehave. But, it still needs to be available for students to see where they stand. Have they lost one privilege or more? Are they still doing well with no accumulated infractions? Following are some examples of tracking systems that provide continuous, visual information about how students are behaving.

We Are Great! Behavior Management Chart

Supplies:

1 large piece of poster board
1 library pocket per student
2 index cards per student
1" (2.54 cm) round stickers: 1 green sticker per student, 3 yellow stickers per student, and 3 red stickers per student
Permanent marker
Glue

Assembling the Index Cards: Hold a card vertically. Place one green sticker in the center of the top edge. Assemble one of these for each student.

Hold the second card vertically. Place one yellow sticker in the center of the top edge and two yellow stickers side-by-side in the center of the bottom edge. Turn over the card. On the back, place one red sticker in the center of the top edge and two red stickers side-by-side in the center of the bottom edge. (See illustration on page 75.) Assemble one of these for each student.

Assembling the Chart: Use a permanent marker to write each child's name on a library pocket. Or, if you prefer to keep the chart anonymous, assign each child a number and number the pockets. Glue the pockets to the poster board in a grid pattern. (See illustration on page 75.) Place two cards in each library pocket. The card with the green sticker should be showing, and the other card should be hidden behind it. You can also use a pocket chart or space on a bulletin board instead of the poster board with library pockets.

Using the Chart: Display the chart on a wall or bulletin board in the back of the room. Make sure it is low enough for all students to reach the library pockets. Begin each day with all of the cards showing green stickers. The goal is to still be "on green" at the end of the day. When you issue the first consequence after the verbal redirect, instruct the student to walk to the chart and put the card with the single yellow sticker in front. Then, he should serve his time out (or whatever the consequence is). For the next consequence, he should flip over his card to show the two yellow stickers. Then, he will serve his consequence. On the next misbehavior, instruct him to turn the card to the single red sticker and serve his consequence. When a student is instructed to turn his card to show the two red stickers, send him to the principal's office. Remember to turn all of the cards back to green before school starts the next morning to indicate a "clean slate."

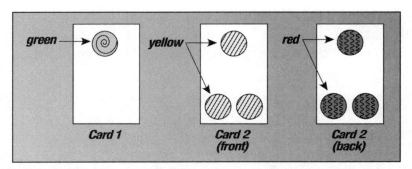

Alternate Behavior Management Display

Supplies:

1 large piece of poster board
1 plastic or plastic foam cup per student
4 colorful craft sticks per student
Permanent marker
Glue or stapler

Preparing the Colorful Craft Sticks: Using the permanent marker, draw a happy face on one end of each craft stick. (See illustration below.)

Assembling the Chart: Write each child's name on a cup with a permanent marker. Or, if you prefer to keep the chart anonymous, assign each child a number and number the cups. Glue or staple the cups to the poster board in a grid pattern. (See illustration below.) Put four craft sticks in each cup. Place an empty cup or basket near the chart.

This chart is similar to the library pocket chart, but each student starts the day with four craft sticks in her cup. Whenever a student receives a consequence after the verbal redirect, she should remove one craft stick from her cup and put it in the nearby container. When a student is instructed to remove the fourth craft stick from her cup, send her to the principal's office. Remember that each student should start the day with four sticks in her cup on the chart. The goal is to keep four sticks all day.

Note: When the entire class finishes the day with four sticks in their cups, it is time for a group reward!

MANAGEMENT STRATEGIES

You have met the families, welcomed the students, completed the icebreakers, introduced classroom customs, and taught the behavior plan and procedures. Now, what else can you do to maintain the order that you have worked so hard to create? This chapter will examine some ideas for maintaining order. In many cases, you can avoid using the behavior plan by redirecting students with one of the following strategies. Let's take a closer look at your main responsibilities in creating a positive classroom community.

Communicate Calmly, Clearly, and with Authority.

Make sure your voice and the look on your face convey that you are calm and in control. For instance, imagine you are preparing to work with a reading group. You have given the class seat work to complete while you are working with the group. You have clearly explained the assignment, answered questions from students to clear up any misunderstandings, and instructed them to begin working on their assignments as you call a reading group to the table. You notice that Matthew is out of his seat talking to another child. Say calmly and evenly, "Matthew, return to your desk and begin your seat work." Turn to the students at the table with you and tell them to open their books to the appropriate page. Now, scan to see if Matthew has complied. If he has, continue with the reading group. If he has not, repeat your direction more firmly and remember to remain calm and collected, "Matthew, return to your desk and begin your seat work."

Return to Teaching as Soon as Possible.

As soon as an off-task student complies, thank her and immediately go back to teaching. Never dwell on one student's misbehavior, especially in front of the class. Always make every effort to return to your normal teaching stance as soon as possible. This gives students a sense of security and allows you to feel more successful in the classroom. It also increases your chances of effectively completing the lesson while minimizing the opportunities for off-task students to absorb time and attention that should be used for advancing the learning of all of the students. Sometimes, teachers become so absorbed with addressing the misbehavior that the whole class gets distracted. Besides increasing the audience for the misbehaving child, this behavior takes valuable learning time from the other class members.

Walk Around the Classroom as You Teach.

Walking around encourages students to follow you with their eyes and shift in their seats, giving them a chance to move a bit and change their focus. This stimulates the brain! As you near students while walking, it is a great time to smile at them to show them how important they are to you. You can also use this time to whisper praise for on-task students or soft redirections to students who might be off task or beginning to disrupt.

Use Verbal Correction.

Avoid Speaking Loudly or through "Gritted Teeth." Raising your voice and showing anger or frustration on your face will often trigger negative reactions from students. Avoid asking inflammatory questions, such as, "Marsha, why are you out of your seat? What should you be doing?" or telling a child what she is doing wrong, "Marsha, you are out of your seat." These are ineffective management strategies, and they invite a child to argue with you as she makes an effort to justify her actions.

When you see a misbehavior that needs to be corrected, quickly check yourself to see that you are calm enough to address the misbehavior. Then, simply call the student by her name and give a direction that specifies exactly what you want her to do.

For example:

"Marsha, sit in your own seat, take out your math book, and start your assignment."

"Sarah, stop talking and complete your assignment."

By specifically stating what you expect the student to be doing, you do not offer an outlet for arguments. If you ask questions, you will receive responses that could escalate into an argument.

If the student does not comply, repeat your direction again calmly. This time, speak even more calmly and insert longer pauses between the words to create more emphasis.

"Marsha, *(pause briefly)* sit in your own seat, *(pause briefly)* take out your math book, *(pause briefly)* and start your assignment."

"Sarah, *(pause briefly)* stop talking, *(pause briefly)* and complete your assignment."

Use the "Hey, You!" Strategy. While you are teaching, mention the off-task student's name to regain his attention. For example, "So, as you can see, Craig, when we mix yellow with blue, we make green. Who can tell me what might happen if we mix yellow with red?"

Most often, the off-task student will return to the task with no more intervention. Hearing his name called aloud alerts him to the need for compliance.

Note: This strategy is very different from one in which the teacher calls upon the off-task student to give an answer. Utilizing this technique runs the risk of escalating the incorrect behavior. The child will be embarrassed in front of his peers because he was not paying attention and does not know the answer. This technique is not effective, and it will hurt your relationship with the student.

Give Students Some Space. Sometimes, a student needs a moment "alone" to decide what to do. So, give the misbehaving student some space to comply without having an audience. For this type of student, state your request, turn away from him, and continue to teach for a couple of minutes. This allows the student to comply without "losing face." If a student feels that he will lose a battle with you, he might be more inclined to continue misbehaving. By turning away, the perceived battle cannot take place. For example, if Jawan is talking to his friend instead of working, you might say, "Jawan, get started with your story. No talking." Then, continue to move around the room monitoring others or completing your task. After a few minutes, look at Jawan again to be sure he chose to comply with your request.

As soon as he complies, give him an appropriate positive response, such as a smile, a thumbs-up, a gentle pat on the shoulder, or a calm "Thank you, Jawan," and continue teaching.

Give Community Praise. This technique not only redirects the off-task student, it also reinforces the behavior of on-task students. When a student is off task, praise one or more of the on-task students who are working near the off-task student. Generally, she will look around, notice what is going on, and begin following directions. When a student is back on task, be sure to capture the opportunity to praise her and her classmates for appropriate behavior. "Way to go, Meredith! Thanks for taking out your science notebook. We have such a wonderful class of learners!"

Use Nonverbal Messages.

Give "The Look." Many students will respond to a nonverbal refocusing statement better than a verbal one. When you need to deliver a nonverbal message, pause momentarily to make sure you are calm, and then deliver "The Look." Students know "The Look." Many parents have one, and teachers do, too. Students know that "The Look" means, "I see you. I know you are not doing what you should be doing. I want you to stop now and return to the task at hand."

How do you develop "The Look"? Make eye contact and calmly look directly at the student. Use a nonthreatening, yet firm, expression that encourages the child to comply. Do not glare at him and grit your teeth with an attitude of anger. This invites hostility from the student and may create a confrontation. A calm, somewhat stern look is effective and nonthreatening. Your calmness will provide the student with an unexpected reaction. He is expecting you to be confrontational. This is an effective way to get his attention and compliance.

Use no words. As soon as the child begins to comply, reward him with a smile or a thumbs-up and move forward with the lesson.

Use Magnetic Movement. Even attentive students are drawn to misbehavior. When a student is off task, others will focus on the misbehavior instead of the task at hand. When using Magnetic Movement to refocus an off-task student, you use proximity to redirect the behavior. Without stopping your lesson, walk calmly and slowly to the off-task student and stand near her for a moment, continuing to teach until the student gets back on task. Bringing the teaching process to that student's area allows you to monitor and redirect her behavior without having to stop the lesson. And, you will not need to use any verbal cues. Your proximity tells the student that you need for her to get back on task. If necessary, place your hand on the edge of the student's desk in order to emphasize the reason for your proximity. She will most likely get back to work. When she does, remember to offer her a smile or signal of positive praise for her compliance.

Use Communicative Gestures. A finger raised to your closed lips reminds a child to stop talking. You can also use a silent signal of "zipping the lips." Avoid saying, "Shhh!" Students quickly learn to ignore this sound and continue with their misbehavior. A firm, but calmly delivered gesture, possibly including the child's name, often helps obtain compliance. Be sure to reward the compliance with a smile and an affirmative nod of your head as you quickly return to your lesson.

Don't Forget to Pay Attention to Positive Behavior, Too.

Sometimes it is so easy to focus on misbehavior that rewarding good behavior is forgotten! Remember not to fall into this trap. It is so important to praise positive behavior because it reinforces students who are on task while reminding off-task students about what they should be doing. In some cases, rewarding positive behavior is the best redirection for misbehavior. Misbehaving students who hear you praising their classmates will feel left out and try to gain your praise by getting back on task. Make sure you recognize this when it happens!

Compliment the Entire Class as Often as Possible.

"Mrs. Bradley's friends, you are doing a great job practicing your alphabet letters. Way to go!"

"Thank you, second graders, for working so quietly."

"Mr. Evans's Owls, I am so pleased with the way you are cooperating in the math center. Keep up the great work!"

Offer Compliments When Students Quickly Comply with Directions. First, give the direction. "Class, please quickly and quietly get your writing folders and bring them to your desks." Then, look around the room for one student who is following your directions. Praise that student aloud. "Jonathan walked right over to the folder box, took out his folder without a sound, and went right back to his seat. Thank you so much, Jonathan!" or, "Thank you, Jonathan, for being such a good member of our community. You've gotten out your folder and are on the right track." This form of praise not only praises the child for compliance but reminds other students what is expected of them, as well.

Recognize the Whole Class While Teaching a Small Group. Be conscious of the entire community at all times. Even when you are working at a table with a small group, keep your eye on the rest of the class. When the class is working independently, they need to be reminded that you notice their excellent behavior. When the tone is just right and you know nearly everyone is working, give the class verbal praise or a point toward a class incentive.

Accentuate the Positive. Use specifics when you offer praise. Rather than just saying, "Thank you" or "Way to go," offer praise for a specific act. By verbalizing specific thanks, you not only give a student praise, you also tell the rest of the class exactly what they should be doing, too. This technique can be used for individuals or for groups. For example, "Monique, today you are working really hard on your science worksheet. Way to go! Our community is proud of you."

It is important to state that the community is proud rather than "you" are proud. It further emphasizes that each person in the classroom community is responsible for and to the other community members.

Praise While Teaching the Entire Class. Stop periodically to praise the class, give them points on the board, or use whatever praise method you have established. Praise individual students—especially difficult students—who are paying attention to the lesson. Catch them being good! A certain number of points on the board should earn a privilege, such as an extra story time, recess, class game, etc. Remember, it must be something that the children really want, or they will not work to earn it.

Offer Spontaneous Privileges. Perhaps the class has a favorite game, book, snack, or movie. As a reward for good behavior, spontaneously stop or complete the activity that they are working on and give them a reward. A reward that is unexpected can be even more fun than one that is planned. A break in the usual schedule is always exciting for students (and for their teacher)! Be sure to tell them why they are getting this reward so that they know how to earn spontaneous privileges again in the future.

Note: Before providing a snack or any food for students, ask families' permission and inquire about students' food allergies and religious or other food preferences.

> Be specific when you offer praise. You are not only giving a student praise, you are also telling the rest of the class exactly what they should be doing, too.

The Ticket to Good Behavior

Use a tangible reward system for good behavior. Keep a supply of tickets on hand to give to students who exhibit good behavior. You can purchase rolls of tickets at office supply stores, or you can make your own using the Ticket Templates (page 84). Give the tickets a name that students will recognize, such as Mrs. Brady's Brag Tags or Terrific Tickets. Keep the tickets with you at all times. Consider wearing a carpenter's apron (available free at most home improvement stores) as an easy way to carry the tickets with you. When you see deserving behavior, give the student a ticket and reward him with a compliment and a specific statement about why he is receiving the ticket.

In addition to good behavior, you should also use the tickets to show your appreciation for random acts of kindness, great work, good grades on tough assignments or tests, a job well-done by a student who struggles in a particular area, or other good efforts. It is also important to recognize students who show major improvement academically or behaviorally. Remember to tell students specifically why they are receiving tickets so that they know what behavior you are reinforcing.

After students receive the tickets, you can have students write their names on their tickets and place them in a large, empty container, such as a fish bowl or coffee can. Then, periodically select a ticket from the container. The student whose ticket you select will receive a reward. Once a quarter, empty the container and start over.

Or, you might choose to use the tickets as a way to encourage responsibility while teaching a lesson about economics. Instead of having students place their tickets in a container, have them keep their tickets in a safe place. Once every two weeks, allow students to use tickets to "purchase" rewards. For example, you might offer a chance to sit at your desk during silent reading time for five tickets. Or, you might also have a "treasure box" filled with items donated by parents or purchased at a discount store that students can purchase with their tickets.

Establish a list of privileges that students can earn with their tickets. Consult with the class about things that they might like to add to the list. Some privileges might include sitting at your desk during a lesson, being line leader, eating lunch with you or with a friend of choice, feeding the class pet for a week, etc.

Ticket Templates

Community Compliment Reward

Hang a long, thick piece of yarn on a bulletin board or another very visible place in the room. Attach one end of the yarn to the top of the board and let the rest of the yarn hang down. Place a box of 15–20 clothespins in a small container near the piece of yarn. Every time an adult spontaneously gives the class a compliment, allow a student to clip a clothespin to the yarn. When all of the clothespins are clipped to the yarn, the class should receive a great reward, such as "Fun Friday," when the last 45 minutes of the day are spent playing favorite class games, reading a favorite story, or watching a video of a story students have read.

Certificates from the Teacher

Students love to receive certificates as rewards for jobs well-done. Use the Certificate Templates (page 86), purchase premade certificates, or create your own. When a student does something that is especially deserving of recognition, complete the certificate and present it to her. Also, consider filling out a certificate and sending it home to the family to notify them of their child's good behavior. This is especially helpful for students who misbehave often. Letting a family know when their child is on the right track is very meaningful!

Certificate Templates

Super Student Award!

Presented to: _____

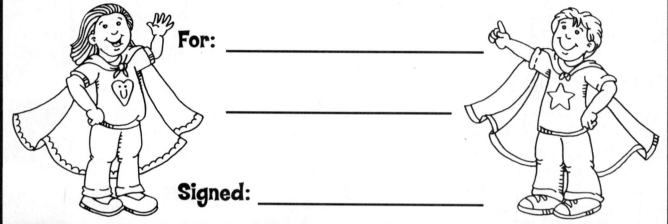

For: _____

_____

Signed: _____

Amazing! Wow! Fantastic!

Presented to: _____

For: _____

Signed: _____ Date: _____

 CD-104117 Creative Classroom Management

Say What You Mean and Mean What You Say!

One of the most important aspects of classroom management is consistency. If students know what to expect from you, they will be more secure in their environment. It is critical that you follow through with discipline techniques and always remain fair and consistent. If you tell a student that she has chosen to miss five minutes of recess, you must remember to deduct that five minutes when recess time arrives. Students need to know that you mean what you say.

Tell Students Exactly What You Expect. If the class is not behaving as you expect them to, get their attention and tell them what they should be doing. For example, if the noise level in the room is too loud, use a quieting technique, such as turning off the lights and singing the "Give Me Five" song (page 48). This will get their attention. After you have their attention, calmly and clearly tell them what behavior you expect at that time. For instance, "Students, mouths are quiet." Make sure your facial expression is calm, not angry. If students see anger on your face, it may challenge some of them to see how much angrier they can make you.

Next, say, "Thank you. The noise level was too high. It is difficult for us to do our best learning when it is loud. Use quiet voices. Thank you." Turn the lights back on and monitor students for compliance as you walk around offering assistance with the task. You have told them exactly what you expect and done it in a way that tells them that you meant what you said.

If noncompliance occurs regularly, take time to reteach the procedure for the expected behavior. Bring out the applicable procedure card and reteach the procedure at that very moment. Have them practice the procedure. If they do not do it correctly, have them practice it again.

If, after a reasonable amount of time, there are still students who choose not to comply, it is imperative that only those who are noncompliant receive the outlined consequences. Avoid punishing the entire class for misbehavior. The children who were following directions know that a whole-class consequence is not fair, and you will damage your relationship with them.

Remember to return to an attitude of joy with the class immediately after consequences have been issued. All correction should be done in a matter-of-fact manner and delivered calmly and clearly. Students learn best in an atmosphere of acceptance and joy.

Show Students Exactly What You Expect. When appropriate, use visual aids to display behavior expectations. In addition to the posted classroom rules, consider posting visual reminders of important behavior expectations, especially for things that might not always be done the same way or things that do not happen on a daily basis. For example, you might use a Noise Level Meter, a Science Experiment Reminder, or a Classroom Visitor Checklist.

A Noise Level Meter is an enlarged image of a stoplight with an arrow or clothespin to point to the expected noise level. For example, if students should be reading silently, put the arrow on the red light labeled "No Talking." If students are working with partners, put the arrow on the yellow light labeled "Whisper Voices." And, if the entire class is working on a lesson together, place the arrow on the green light labeled "Raise Your Hand to Speak." These are, of course, just examples of how your stoplight might be labeled, but it gives students a specific visual representation of your expectations.

A Science Experiment Reminder and a Classroom Visitor Checklist are visual reminders of your expectations during a science experiment or when a visitor is in the room. Sometimes, students will become especially excited when something new and different is on the schedule, such as a new experiment or a visitor. Before these activities occur, remind students of your expectations and post them in a visible place. For younger students, consider adding illustrations to the list. Any time you are preparing for something special that is not part of the regular routine, consider making a visual reminder as a "temporary procedure" lesson.

Arguing and Manipulation

Never Argue with a Student. When a student tries to argue with you, do not address the argumentative comment. Engaging in the dispute gives him the attention he really wants but generally does not result in compliance. Often, the student can and will come back with an argument that gets a reaction from the class and provides him with the attention he craves.

Use the Refocusing Technique. The refocusing technique will allow you to avoid his attempts to manipulate you.

1. Determine exactly what you want from the student. (If you have procedures in place, students will already be aware of what is expected.)

2. When a student tries to sidetrack you, stay focused on your goal. Repeat your "statement of want" a maximum of three times. Each time speak more slowly and in a lower tone. The student will generally cooperate by this time.

3. Offer a consequence for noncompliance. If the student still refuses to comply with your wishes, give a simple direction and provide a consequence. Note that when you offer the choice of compliance or a consequence, you must follow through. The student will make his choice, and you will either deliver the consequence or reward the compliance.

Following are two scripted examples:

Derek calls out to answer a question without first raising his hand and waiting to be called on.

Teacher: Derek, I want you to raise your hand and wait to be called on before you speak. *(statement of want)*

Derek: None of the other kids do. *(sidetracking attempt)*

Teacher: I hear what you are saying. What I want YOU to do is raise your hand. *(refocusing technique)*

Derek: You never call on me. *(sidetracking attempt)*

Teacher: I understand you feel that way, Derek, but right now I need you to raise your hand and wait for me to call on you before answering. *(refocusing technique)*

Derek: OK. OK. *(Acceptance)*

   In this case, the teacher never needed to offer a consequence.

In the following example, the teacher needs to offer a consequence.

Teacher: Derek, stop talking and return to your seat. (*statement of want*)

Derek: I wasn't talking! You are just picking on me. (*sidetracking attempt*)

> Do not address either of these assertions, especially the "just picking on me" comment. This engages you in his manipulation and starts an argument between the two of you—with the entire class as an audience. Instead, repeat your request in a calm voice.

Teacher: I hear what you are saying, Derek, but I need you to stop talking and return to your seat. (*refocusing technique*)

> Many children avoid compliance because they think they can argue their way out of it. The simple repeating of your request every time he tries to redirect the conversation eliminates his ability to manipulate you into an argument and take your focus off the need for compliance. Again, by not asking questions, you do not invite a combative reply. If you do not engage in the argument, one cannot begin.

> For increased success in diffusing arguing, remember to say the words more slowly and lower your tone each time you repeat your request.

Derek: But, I just need to tell Joey one thing. It's important! You never let us do what we want to do. (*sidetracking attempt*)

> If he still refuses to comply after you have repeated your redirection statement two or three times, state the consequence that he can "choose."

Teacher: Derek, if you do not stop talking and return to your seat, you will choose to stand beside me for the first five minutes of recess. (*offering consequence*)

Derek: But, I just need one minute! (*sidetracking attempt*)

Teacher: Derek, you have chosen to stand beside me for the first five minutes of recess. (*delivering the consequence*)

> The teacher offered the consequence that Derek could CHOOSE. Then, he chose to accept the consequence rather than comply with the teacher's request.

> The calmer you are and the more you avoid engaging in their arguments, the more successful you will be. You will be in control of the situation.

IT'S NOT WORKING; NOW WHAT?

Ideally, all of your hard work and planning will pay off with a perfect school year that is void of any disciplinary problems. However, we all know that this is rarely the case. It is likely, though, that your work to implement this plan will be effective and produce a very positive environment for the majority of the classroom community. If you have followed the plan correctly and consistently while offering a caring and supportive environment for students, you should find yourself able to manage the behavior of a very high percentage of the class with ease.

It is true that there are some students in each class who, due to outside circumstances, do not respond to the plan as it is designed. Your efforts to socialize this type of student may seem fruitless to you. Do not despair! There is a plan for this type of student. It simply calls for a special plan instead of the usual group plan.

Before you design a special plan, check to make sure you have applied all of the appropriate techniques from your regular plan. Assess the situation by completing the Assessing Your Management Skills checklist (page 92). Rating yourself honestly in each area will either provide you with a reminder of some strategies you have not yet utilized or assure you that you have done everything you normally do to successfully manage students' behavior. If you find the latter to be true, it is an indication that you do, indeed, need to design new strategies for the specific student.

> When the plan is in place, you should be able to manage a very high percentage of the class with ease. But, there are some students in each class who, due to outside circumstances, do not respond to the plan as it is designed.

Assessing Your Management Skills

Assessing Your Management of a Particular Student

Use this checklist to determine if you have successfully completed all of the steps of your plan with a student who misbehaves regularly.

Have you . . .

1. _____ delivered clear directions in a calm manner?

2. _____ taught—not just talked about—the expected behavior, questioned for understanding, and had the student practice the correct behavior?

3. _____ utilized positive reinforcement, such as compliments and rewards?

4. _____ asked the student's family for input as soon as problems surfaced?

5. _____ provided one-on-one time to try to find out what might be behind the repeated misbehavior, such as lack of sleep, issues at home, misconceptions, etc.?

6. _____ consistently administered a consequence or redirection every time the student has been disruptive or off task?

7. _____ provided consequences in a calm, matter-of-fact manner without judgment or sarcasm?

8. _____ offered praise or clarification about the student's performance of procedures?

9. _____ contacted family members regularly to keep them informed about improvements and problems?

10. _____ given the student a "clean slate" every day?

CD-104117 Creative Classroom Management

Creating a Special Plan

When you have tried all of your usual strategies and none of them seem to successfully reach a certain student, it is time to devise a special plan to tap into that student's strengths and address his particular needs for attention or control. The plan you create will supersede the Classroom Community Behavior Plan for this individual child and you will focus on a plan that will meet his specific needs.

First, brainstorm ideas that you believe might help this child succeed as a community member. Next, seek the counsel of other staff members in the school who can encourage you and provide valuable input. While you may seek such advice from other classroom teachers, also remember to seek advice from anyone who might have a relationship with the student, including lunchroom assistants, librarians, counselors, coaches, and music, art, and physical education teachers. Also, talk with the student's family to find adults outside of the school who might be helpful, such as scout troop leaders, youth group leaders, camp counselors, etc. It is very helpful to get input from a variety of people in the student's community.

Problem-Solving Conference

Take the notes you have created into a problem-solving conference. You will hold this conference on an individual basis with the student to assemble a plan for her success. If you feel it will be helpful, invite a family member to attend the meeting. It may be more fruitful for you to talk one-on-one with the student. Or, consider meeting with the student alone first, then invite a family member to join you. You and the student can share the new plan with the family member. This will allow the student to take ownership of the plan and acknowledge that she will work to improve her behavior. Use your judgment to decide which meeting format will yield the best results.

Be prepared with a list of possible positives and consequences that will be effective for the specific student. For example, if the student seems to strongly seek attention, perhaps offering to sit with her during lunch would be just the reward she needs for good behavior. Or, have you noticed that she always stops misbehaving before she receives consequence number four (a phone call home)? Maybe that is because a phone call home is the most effective consequence for her. In her plan, the phone call home should be the first consequence after the verbal redirect.

Plan the conference at a time when you can give the student your undivided attention, preferably after school, before school starts, or during lunch. It is very important that you not have any disruptions or distractions during this meeting.

Whether you choose to invite family members to the meeting, let them know about it and keep them posted about the results. It is a good idea to send this information in the form of a letter so that there is a written record of the plan.

Conducting the Meeting

Begin with a positive declaration, such as, "Marissa, we're having this talk because I care about you and really want you to succeed in our community and be happy. You're an important member of our community, and we all need your help."

Clearly and calmly tell the student why the conference is taking place. For example, "Marissa, lately you have been yelling at your classmates and calling them names." Only name one or two misbehaviors. It is important to focus on a reasonable number of behaviors to extinguish first. This gives the student a clear focus. As she achieves success in these two areas, it will not seem as daunting to expand the process to include additional behaviors. You will be able to praise the way the previous behaviors have been diminished or eliminated and assure the student that she can also be successful in these areas.

Do not ask why she does the things that she does. There probably is not a good answer to justify the behavior, so don't ask the question.

Ask what she thinks the other students think about her behavior. How does she feel about the effect her behavior has on her classmates?

Ask how she feels about the consequences she has to serve when she chooses to misbehave. If you receive a response like, "I don't care," be sure to reply with a statement that expresses how much you and the classroom community care. Staying calm and positive with the student will assist her in de-escalating. Do not let her make you flustered or agitated when she uses argumentative statements. If you do not engage in an argument, it cannot begin.

Ask what you can do to help. The purpose of this question is to ascertain whether the student has a perspective that you have not yet seen. For example, she may say something like, "I sit beside Mark, and all he does is laugh at me when I make a mistake, and you never catch him." This gives you insight that tells you to do three things: heighten your observance of Mark and his behavior, consider moving the student away from Mark, and remind her that she is responsible for her own actions and responses to others. Always express your belief in her ability to change her behavior in a positive way.

Encourage the child to talk with you and not give one-word answers. Tell her that you want to hear her side. Tell her that you think what she thinks is important because you care for her and want things to be better for her. Remind her that she is important to you.

Also tell her how important she is to the classroom community. She may act like this is not important to her, but it is. Everyone wants to know that others care. It is important to her self-esteem.

Together, choose two important agreements that you want her to focus on, such as following directions and keeping her hands, feet, and objects to herself.

Express your confidence in her ability to successfully follow the rules. Your warm expression of confidence can begin to change her negative beliefs about herself into positive ones.

Together, fill in the Community Assistance Contract (page 96). It is called the Community Assistance Contract because it outlines what the student can do personally to assist the entire community in reaching its goals.

After you have filled in the form together, have the student sign it with you. If you have invited family members to join the meeting, bring them in now. Ask the student to share the plan with them. Go over the form together and make copies for you, the student, and the family members. Keep your copy in her file. Hopefully, this meeting will be just what she needs to realize that you care enough to work specifically with her to meet her needs while she works to help the class meet its goals. Again, remember to administer the positives and consequences of this plan in the same way that you administer the positives and consequences for the rest of the class. Consistency is key!

> **Administer the positives and consequences of this plan in the same way that you administer the positives and consequences for the rest of the class. Remember, consistency is key!**

Community Assistance Contract

Student's Name: _____

Date of Conference: _____

Reason for the Conference: Our class needs _____'s help to be
the best that it can be!

1. Which rule(s) is being broken? _____

2. What is the student doing, specifically, to break the rule(s)? _____
   _____

3. What can the community, including the teacher, do to help the student be

   more successful? _____

   _____

4. What can the student do to help the community be more successful? _____

   _____

5. How would the student like to celebrate when he or she accomplishes the goals of

   this plan? (a special community privilege or treat, a note home, etc.) _____

   _____

6. What are some fair consequences for times when the student chooses to break

   the rules? _____

   _____

7. How does the student think the community will feel about his or her contributions

   to classroom success? _____

   _____

By signing below, we pledge to do our very best to make our classroom community the
best it can be!

Student's Signature: _____

Teacher's Signature: _____

CD-104117 Creative Classroom Management